New Beginnings

ALYSHA SMITH

New Beginnings
Copyright © 2020 by Alysha Smith

All rights reserved. No part of this publication may be
reproduced, distributed, or transmitted in any form or
by any means, including photocopying, recording, or
other electronic or mechanical methods, without the prior
written permission of the author, except in the case of
brief quotations embodied in critical reviews and certain
other non-commercial uses permitted by copyright law.

Tellwell Talent
www.tellwell.ca

ISBN
978-0-2288-2525-8 (Hardcover)
978-0-2288-2524-1 (Paperback)
978-0-2288-2526-5 (eBook)

This is Me

Hello, beautiful people. I'm so excited that you are choosing to tune in and join me on this journey. I'll define this read as a self-help/memoir because I speak to circumstances that have occurred in my life along with life lessons, gratitude, and wisdom learned along the way. I'm sharing this information with you in hopes that you will become inspired about your own journey and your calling in life. I would like to remind you that you're human and deserve a wonderful life full of love. I believe that you picked up this book for a reason. I'm not sure what that reason is, but since you have given it a chance, I hope you find your "AHA!" moment within. Your time is valuable, and so I hope you find some useful/inspiring information to walk away with. This book is my New Beginning, and I hope can be a supporter of yours. I am giving you a clear warning/disclaimer: for those who get offended easily and dislike the use of vulgar language, this book will challenge you. My book found its way into your hands, so you must be in need of a message or two within the chapters you're about to read. If you're standing in the store debating on buying it or not, or if you've already bought the damn thing, go with your gut. If your gut says stick with it, you might get a chuckle every now and again if you have an open mind. I will be unpacking some real shit about motherhood, abandonment, life, struggles, goals, and opportunities. I am blunt as hell; I say it like it is, but it's all in the hopes that I can grab your attention so you can walk away with a newfound understanding of yourself.

My memories are imperfect, but the events portrayed in this book are to the best of my knowledge. While the stories in this book are my truths, some names and identifying details have been changed to protect the identity and privacy of the people involved. I recognize that the individuals I speak about may have a different view about the memories of the events that took place. I want to honour this and state that this book is not intended to hurt anyone. This book is for entertainment purposes and I cannot be held responsible for the way in which the reader interprets the content.

Most humans desire to find passionate, unconditional love; get married; have children, work to provide and retire; and live by the "norms of society." I like to consider myself a bit of a rebel, as I don't tend to follow the norms of society. I had a baby before I got married (slap on the wrist, bad Alysha to some of you reading); I spent money on attending university but crave an opportunity to work for myself and ditch the degree. No, I am not saying that people shouldn't attend post-secondary education, but I am saying that people should follow their crazy dreams and the fire in their heart. This book is jam-packed with relatable and real stories that are outside of the "social norms." I am god-awful honest because let's face it: it's tough to find honesty nowadays. Everyone seems to pretend that they are living the Kardashian lifestyle on social media to gain attention rather than living for themselves and BEING themselves. I AM WHO I AM, and I am sharing some of my vulnerable stories with you in the hopes that you learn something.

In my twenty-six years of existence, I have learned to not give a fuck about what people think or say about me (this is extremely hard to do, and I didn't learn this skill overnight). Everyone is entitled to an opinion; however, it is up to that individual to choose whether or not those opinions will run and rule their life.

Not giving a fuck about what people think and say about me allows me to live in my reality, in my world, while blocking out external nonsense. In my world, I don't have regrets, only gained knowledge and experiences that help me grow to become the best version of myself. My hope for you as a reader is that you will take away what you need to. For some, this book might be similar to AA or a "quick fix," and for others, you may want to burn this book and never speak of it again. Regardless, I respect and value the time you are taking to read it. I just want to ensure that I provide you with fair warning. There may be content in this book that will trigger some audiences. If you are using this book as an aid to support you through your own personal conflicts, then please reach out for support whether that be from a friend, a partner, or a medical professional if need be. I am not a doctor, I am not a therapist, I am not above you or below you. I am a fucking human being, just like you, who is simply living out my purpose of motiving and supporting others along their journeys.

While you read, I want you to think about what you're waiting for in life. Life is too damn short to wait for permission from your lover, for advice from your teacher, or for Santa Claus to come down the fucking chimney and hand you a promising life on Christmas morning. I have some news for ya'll: YOU, and only you, are in charge of your life. You get to make your decisions — not your parents, not society. Please don't try to live a life to please others; you will feel miserable and resentful and most of all unhappy. Just a little piece of friendly advice: we aren't promised a tomorrow, so if you have goals, dreams, places you want to travel, and things you crave to do in this lifetime, then make them a priority, make them happen. You are the only one standing in your way. Everyone is entitled to their own opinions, but let those opinions remain insignificant to your life and your way of existing on this Earth. "Do what you love and love what you do" – Dr. John Demartini. Find your inner peace, love yourself, and let go of the idea of needing to please people or live your life for others.

People will have their opinions; it's inevitable. People will view the world in a completely different form than you do, and that's okay; just let it be. If you would like to hear my suggestion, I encourage you to be respectful, always remain true to your authentic self, and remember that the opinions of others are their truths, not yours. You have the power to accept or reject the opinions of others. It does take practice, but if conserving your energy means something to you, then you can try saying "thanks for sharing your thoughts" and walk away. Some people are searching for an emotional response from you. It's up to you whether or not you provide it. You could also just kill them with kindness. In my experience, it is challenging for people to fight with or gain an emotional reaction from someone who remains calm and kind.

> If someone tells me the sky is green, I simply say, okay. I do not need to agree with them or prove them wrong or show them proof that I am right. I simply go on with my life with a newfound understanding that to some people the sky looks green and I am okay with that. It keeps external conflicts from disturbing my inner peace and isn't that where world peace begins, with each of us finding peace? – Timber Hawkeye

Abandonment

"Definition: the action or fact of abandoning or being abandoned leaving one to feel undesired, left behind, discarded or insecure." – Urban Dictionary

Life is all about perspective. I'm sure you have heard the phrase about the glass being either half-full or half-empty. But what if you looked at that glass as either a missed or gained opportunity, depending on your perspective and how you choose to view situations in your life? Time for some personal stories (we all love this shit). For me, my first-time experiencing abandonment was when a significant person in my life decided to move elsewhere to build a new life for themselves. I was ten and I viewed this person as my world. This person went from being one of my heroes to a non-existent stranger in a flash. I often have thoughts about the positive memories we lived through together and I reminisce about the beautiful moments we shared as opposed to the abandonment itself. Of course, the act of abandonment took a toll on me emotionally and mentally and it was tough for ten-year-old Alysha to accept. As a little girl, I thought that in order to be loved, this love had to be provided by certain people that I could count on for anything and everything. I eventually learned that love could come from many different places and many different people and I realized that my "cup" was being filled and overflowed by love from everyone else around me. When I was twenty-three years old, I learned that forgiveness was a crucial component in the healing process. I didn't know that it was possible to have love for someone who had hurt me. I will explore this in detail later. I just want everyone reading to know this, repeat this, and live by this: If someone you love has left your life, it is for a reason and you did nothing to cause it. The individual was most likely struggling with a battle of their own.

I experienced another major loss in my early adult years while still completing my course in university. This person was another significant individual in my life who decided to venture on to their own journey. This loss left me feeling pretty fucked up emotionally. I remember struggling so badly with my emotions that yes, thoughts of suicide existed. No, I did not have a plan for suicide, but I did have some dark thoughts about how life would be easier if mine ended. I admit that I had dark thoughts and I felt broken, BUT I did not let the thoughts consume me. I decided that I was not going to let the feelings of abandonment win. I marched my ass down to my school counsellor and attended sessions to release my feelings and my bottled-up anger/pain. I told my counsellor that I felt broken. My counsellor did something that to this day still impacts me when I think about it. She stopped me, grabbed a pencil, broke the pencil in half, and said, "A pencil is an inanimate object that can snap and break. You are a human. You are not broken. You are stuck, and I am here to help you." I instantly cried as I let those words process in my brain. From this point on, I decided to view life as a bundle of opportunities waiting for me to find them. I decided that everything happens for a reason. I decided that my mental, emotional, and physical health matters. For anyone who is struggling with their mental health, thoughts of suicide, or feelings of loneliness and depression, you are not alone and you matter. Mental health is not something to fuck around with. There are resources available and people who love you. You are a human being on this Earth and your existence matters. To me (a complete stranger), you MATTER.

So, with this abandonment throughout my childhood, I often felt insecure, I lacked self-esteem, and I accepted attention from those who would provide it. These acts of abandonment led me to search for a sense of belonging in my relationships, friendships, and interactions. I found myself entering into romantic relationships from the young age of fifteen and believing with all my heart that each relationship was "the love of my life" and the person I would marry. I am not ashamed to admit that I was and continue to be fearful of being alone, because to me being alone means being unwanted, forgotten, and undesired. I craved a sense of belonging with a male figure so badly that I jumped from relationship to relationship. The interesting piece (I'm diving into the WHYs) is that I have always been the one to end my relationships. My pattern is "jump in and get the fuck out when things start to go south." This is and has always been my own form of protection. In my own reality, I say things like, "Okay, Alysha, things are looking down, so prepare and get out of that before they have the opportunity to abandon you." In a sense, I abandon the ugly situation before they have an opportunity to abandon me. It's fucked, right? I'm still trying to figure myself out, but I'm willing to share this process with the world in order to get you thinking about your own patterns, your own self-sabotage, your own baggage. I have realized at the age of twenty-six that I need to stop looking outward and start looking inside of my being for happiness. One of my biggest life lessons to date has been: "No one can make you happy, PERIOD. You need to find contentment within yourself before you can give all of yourself to another human being. Look within; you possess all of the answers you need inside of you."

Although I have had my fair share of relationships, I do not regret any of them because I continued to grow as a person and recognize in each the aspects of a relationship that I desired and the aspects I disliked. I am taking this opportunity to thank my exes because I wouldn't be the person I am today without the experiences that brought me here.

I take a huge interest in the psychology of the brain. This section might seem random, but bear with me: there is a purpose. Children's brains are like tiny computers and they work to gather information in order to process. What children witness in their lives at young ages can result in the decisions they make as young adults. For example, for a child whose parent remarries multiple times, jumping from relationship to relationship might seem "normal." Your parents are kind of like the role models of your world who help shape what yours might look like. You may say things like, "Well, Dad did it, so it must be normal and okay." I'm not downing anyone who has entered into multiple relationships or remarried, by the way. Life is all about trial and error and there is nothing wrong with figuring out who you are and who you love along the way.

When children experience traumatic events in their lives such as abandonment, continuous arguments between parents, or abuse of any form, this can cause the brain to become wired to respond to these events in certain ways. Have you heard the term fight or flight? You either run away from your problems or you fight them head on (oftentimes in negative ways). The abandonment that I experienced as a child led me to avoid and run from problems in my life instead of facing them. I have only recently learned to speak up for myself and face issues head on. The desperation for a sense of belonging in my life made it okay for me to enter into multiple relationships with men to seek comfort. I always ensured that I had a relationship to feel "secure" about my own insecurities. My abandonment as a child made me question my worth, it made me jealous in my relationships as a young woman, it made me insecure about myself, and it left me feeling as though I needed to rely on someone to complete the pieces of me that felt incomplete. I could never allow myself to be alone and "single" long enough to learn that I didn't need a romantic partner to "complete me" or to keep me feeling secure. If we are looking for relationships to complete us, then we are entering into relationships for the wrong reasons and they will most likely end. We should not be looking for someone to show us what love is. We should learn to love ourselves on our own and in our own time first.

The point I am trying to make is this: little Alysha experienced abandonment multiple times throughout her life along with witnessing some emotional abuse by some adults around her. This absolutely had an impact on my developing brain and it taught me to seek relationships for support and comfort instead of seeking this within myself. Michelle Obama explained something that strongly resonates with me. She told her audience in her Becoming tour that she was raised with a positive, supportive, active father figure which in turn set the bar high for the partner that she chose for herself. Her partner needed to meet a certain standard. Michelle grew up with empowerment and esteem instilled in her from a young age which supported her with choosing Barack as her partner. The environment in which one grows up can have an effect on the person you are. The loss that I experienced as a child often left me feeling confused and unsure of who I was; this wasn't helpful when searching for a partner. Me choosing a partner in my teen years and my young adult years was about "completing me" and making me feel "whole," which I realize now is not the purpose for any relationship we enter into. We need to learn how to make ourselves whole and love ourselves deeply before we can allow our hearts to extend outwards and love another being. If I could rewind and give the old Alysha a piece of friendly advice, it would be this: Don't search and settle for the first person who shows up to give you attention. Dig within yourself, get to know yourself, put yourself first, and love yourself deeply before you dive headfirst into anything.

The younger Alysha would have done anything to satisfy the empty void within her, even if it meant living outside of her true values in an attempt to seek happiness. An example is committing to someone (the wrong person for me) for the rest of my life because of a beautiful diamond presented to me. I was young, I was naïve, and I wasn't honest or true to myself. I was selfish and agreed to be with someone based on a fantasy I had created in my head. This wasn't fair for the individual or myself, but I absolutely said yes for all of the wrong reasons. The feelings of wanting to be loved and accepted were so intense that without hesitation I agreed to marry the first person who asked me. This person was incredible, by the way, but this just wasn't the right person for me. This experience along with others taught me that no one can make me happy except me. Only I have the power and the ability to make myself happy. Now, anyone who enters into my life is entering to grow with me as a person. I am no longer fearful of hurting people's feelings or following people's orders. I am finally at a place in my life where I can tell people how it is. If they don't like it, there is the door, and I'm moving forward. It took a lot of strength and a long time to reach this point. Ladies, you don't need a man to complete you. Like I said, I don't have regrets for the individuals that I chose to have a romantic relationship with because it helped shape the person I am today. I will just give my daughter this advice: "Learn to make yourself happy, and don't rely on another human being to solve your problems or make you feel whole."

The abandonment that I experienced led me to grieve the loss of many important people in my life. For any child, losing someone through death, loss of connection, or loss of relationship is heartbreaking. I couldn't understand what I did to deserve all this loss. It ate at me, and some days it consumed me. Ten-year-old Alysha was left feeling abandoned without really even knowing what abandonment meant at the time. Questions would run through my mind: "Are they ever coming back?", "Does this mean I'm not worth loving?", and "What did I do to drive them away?" These questions never left my brain until I began my journey of healing and gave myself permission to release my baggage in order to move forward.

When I was twenty-three years old, after I had moved to another province, I finally overcame and accepted the loss of the individuals who had abandoned me. I enrolled in a course called the Breakthrough Experience with one of my mentors Dr. John Demartini. I gave this two-thousand-dollar-course a shot, and boy was I fucking glad I did. I am not going to sit here and beg you to sign up for this course, but I will tell you that it was the most eye-opening, unfuckingbelievable experience I have ever had, and I cannot put into writing the sense of relief and release that was gained. This one weekend course led me to free my soul of the weight it had been carrying throughout my life regarding the abandonment I had experienced. The sense of abandonment no longer consumed me, it no longer controlled me, and it no longer affected me because I found forgiveness and love in my healing. I know some of you must be thinking, "Okay, this course sounds too good to be true." Here is an explanation of the course taken directly from Dr. John Demartini's website (https://drdemartini.com/):

> Created by Dr John Demartini, the Breakthrough Experience is the culmination of 44 years of interdisciplinary study where you will be introduced to two powerful processes, the Demartini Method and the Demartini Value Determination Process. The Breakthrough Experience will provide you with powerful solutions to help you resolve fear, depression, resentment, anger, intimidation, low self-esteem, guilt, grief or anxiety and any emotion you'd love to have stop 'running' your life. This program will get you past your self-imposed limitations so you can develop your true potential, empower all

areas of your life and achieve even more than you
may once have thought possible.

If you are grieving the loss of someone, or if you struggle to appreciate people for who they are and what they have to offer, I strongly recommend looking into this course, and if not this course, then therapy or something else to support your healing journey. Please, I am begging you, please don't sit in pain. Whatever happened to you is shitty, and you didn't deserve any of it, but please don't waste your life away feeling sorry for yourself. Life after healing is beautiful. Take it from someone who has been there.

As a twenty-six-year-old version of myself writing this, I can honestly say that I am grateful for the individuals who walked away. If I saw them walk through the door right now, I would put my arms around them and thank them for making the choice to leave. I AM the person I am today because of my life experiences. I AM who I am today because I chose to take a chance, to take my emotions and life aspirations seriously, and to register for that course. I broke through my barriers, and I am left feeling gratitude in my heart. Here's the bottom line: if you are struggling with shit that has happened to you throughout your life, you have two choices. One, you could let it control you and your emotions and go through the motions of life being miserable; or two, you could make the decision to beat the bullshit that has happened, however you choose to do so, and then find a way to live your best damn life without letting anything or anyone stop you. I could have easily chosen to channel my inner struggling emotions and turn to drugs or alcohol to help numb the pain. I could have made the decision to take my own life. I could have easily made the decision to run away from my problems, but instead, I chose to work through the pain, to really sit in my pain and process it and then free it, free my soul, and find gratitude.

We are all one decision away from a totally different life. Isn't it scary to think that one decision can alter your life so profoundly? And life is full of decisions, so how do we know if we are making the right ones? I choose to listen greatly to this little thing called intuition. We as humans determine our own paths in life. We can choose to dwell on the shit that has happened and play victim, or we can choose to learn from what has happened and live every day to the fullest, accepting that tomorrow might not come, but being exceptionally satisfied with our life if it doesn't. Sometimes we don't understand why things happen to us. We don't understand why we lose loved ones. We don't understand why we must deal with grief and loss. It's important to note that everyone will deal with grief and loss differently, and that is okay. There is no timeline on how long you should grieve. There is no chart to tell you how to feel while you are grieving. But let me say this. If you feel angry (because I have), if you feel resentful (because I have), if you feel like the world has done you wrong and it owes you something (because I have), then I'm asking you to make one of two choices: sit and waste your life away pitying yourself, OR work through your pain, your grief, and your loss and allow yourself to heal and live an extravagant life.

Lesson number one: You did nothing wrong. You were the innocent child. This act of abandonment helped shape the magnificent person you are today. Listen closely: you do not owe anyone anything. YOU get to decide whether or not this "act of abandonment" is going to ruin you or grow you as a person. I choose growth every time because I am the ruler of MY life and I choose what stays and what hits the dusty old trail.

In and Out

Have you ever wondered why some people come into your life and others leave? I truly believe that it is your soul adapting, learning, growing, cleansing, and making room for new and refreshing people. Sometimes we are uncertain about why people leave or why people come. This uncertainty may us feeling angry, disappointed, or confused. I challenge you to start paying attention to the people who enter into your life and the people who exit, and then ask yourself WHY. What is the universe trying to teach me, provide me, or release me from? I like to think of relationships as contracts. When relationships become intolerable or toxic, or when we find ourselves putting more work into the relationship than the other, and we choose to end the relationship, I consider this breaking the contract. Breaking the contract with a friend, a significant other, a parent, a teacher, etc. does not mean that it is broken for good. It is just broken for the moment, and the contract can be renewed and replenished if you choose to do so.

I have had many friendships begin and end, but I find it interesting that the people I continue to attract in my adult years are people who are like-minded. These people leave me feeling refreshed and inspired. I believe that these people are a part of my journey, my story, and I value what each relationship offers. I have watched many of my friendships and relationships dissolve over time, which I think is only natural given that humans are constantly evolving and changing with each passing day. Interests and hobbies change, mindsets and perspectives shift, and if you're anything like me, as you age you stop putting up with nonsense and massive amounts of bullshit. I one hundred per cent believe that what we think about ourselves, we attract. So, if we continue to think "My life is shitty," or "I never save money," then the universe will continue to leave us without money. In other words, we will continue with the same habit for spending instead of saving and we will continue to attract unpleasant events into your life that are perceived as negative. "Our inner thoughts become our outer realities" – Dr. John Demartini. I have learned to believe in myself so gravely and so deeply that the haters of the world can't stop me. I have chosen to surround myself with people who lift me up, who challenge me to think differently, who cheer me on, and who accept me. I have chosen to let go of or break contracts with people who choose to remain stuck in their own life, people who consistently say poor me, people who see themselves as a victim instead of a survivor, and people who place blame on others. Note: these are my boundaries, you can create your own.

I need you to hear that I too have also placed blame on others and I have played a victim at some points in my life; however, I quickly realized that it wasn't getting me ahead. It was setting me back and keeping me stuck, so I asked myself what needed to change and the answer was my perspective. Don't be afraid to accept that you are a human who will make a lot of mistakes along the way, but DO NOT sit in self-pity, because people will eventually stop attending the pity party.

Listen up, people: the universe will place people on your path for a reason. The universe will provide you with what you need if you allow it and if you choose to listen. When you come across someone, and I'm saying when, not if, because you will come across someone in your lifetime who touches your soul, don't overlook it. Embrace it and accept that this is the universe working in your favour. Trust that whoever is meant to be in your life at any given time has a purpose for being there. Trust that at any given moment, relationships and friendships can also crumble, and in those tough moments, trust that the universe has a reason behind this plan. Sometimes we will never know why people come and go. I have chosen to accept and trust in the timing of the universe and that so long as I believe in myself and have my own back, I am not alone. I'm telling you that although you may have days where you feel alone, you are not. Trust in the process; the universe is on your side.

Humans are naturally born with every characteristic: good, bad, angry, happy, humble, cruel, reliable, unreliable, honest, and dishonest to name a few. As mentioned in the previous chapter, one's perspective is key. If I always considered myself to be happy without sad, honest without dishonest, and compassionate without cruel, then I would be living in an unbalanced, unrealistic reality. Whether we like to admit it or not, we have all been cruel, we have all been sad, and we have all been dishonest. But we have also all, at some point, been happy, compassionate, and honest. This makes us human; this makes us whole; this makes us perfectly imperfect. The point I am trying to make is that we need to learn how to have balance. We need to accept that humans are not one-sided and that we all come with a buttload of emotions and characteristics that make up the human race. Change your perspective instead of trying to change people, and appreciate those who are on the journey of life with you.

I want to take this opportunity to thank the universe for providing me with these beautiful souls:

❖ Makayla, you are my soul sister. I feel like I have known you my entire life, yet I only met you in my adult years. The universe needed us to meet, and I cannot thank you enough for your constant support, your understanding, your ear to listen to me vent, and your knowledge. Girl, you are so inspirational and you're going to move mountains.

❖ Shasily, you are the purest soul I have ever met. I cannot thank the universe enough for placing you on my path. You are so vibrant and spread sunshine everywhere you go. The world needs more people like you. Thank you for being you and inspiring me on a daily basis. To my readers, if you ever have a chance to meet this powerful woman, your soul will be left feeling light, inspired, and pure. Shasily, you are absolutely fucking amazing, and you have impacted me more than you know.

❖ PM, you have always provided me with massive amounts of love. You challenge me and you pick me up when I'm feeling low. I have loved watching you blossom into the woman you are today. You're such a caring, inspirational woman and I'm so excited for you to leave your mark on the world.

❖ Mariam, you have always accepted me for who I am. You are a bright, adventurous soul and I love your no-bullshit attitude. I am living through you while you travel the world. Continue to create memories and as you make your wildest dreams come true, my girl!

❖ Paige, you have ventured on this journey of life with me the longest, my love. You have been there for me through thick and thin in our most challenging university years. You hold a special place in my heart and I'm so proud of the woman you have become. Thank you for teaching me that it is okay to whip my hair and dance like no one is watching.

Thank you all for making such an impact on my life and all of the lives you touch every day. You all have a way of balancing me. I believe that we seek out people in our lives (friends, lovers, etc.) to make up for the pieces that we lack. So, if you have some true people who are dear to your heart, send them a text right now, or pick up the phone and just let them know that they are appreciated in every sense.

I also want to thank the individuals who have come on to my path but who had to leave for whatever reason. You are all worthy and deserving of my love and forgiveness. I appreciate what each and every one of you offered me when you were a part of my journey. I have so much love to give. I am choosing to give my love to those who may have hurt me, to those who left my side, and to those who put me down because I recognize now that it was never about me. I believe every single person on this planet is enough and is deserving of love, so you have mine.

Lesson number two: Consider the way people treat you, but most importantly <u>how you let them treat you.</u> Contracts (relationships) can be broken and then renewed when the timing feels right. Thank the universe for placing and removing people on your journey. Your soul needs to be surrounded by positive energy and constant love; you deserve it.

You Aren't for Me

> *"Definition: A **toxic relationship** is often characterized by repeated, mutually destructive modes of relating between two people. These patterns can involve jealousy, possessiveness, dominance, manipulation, desperation, selfishness or rejection." – Urban Dictionary*

Throughout life, you will meet people you vibe with and people you take no interest in pursuing a relationship with. You will also come across relationships that take a shitload of work to make last, relationships that challenge who you are as a person and possibly relationships that are down right toxic. I'm not here to tell you who you should or shouldn't have relationships with in your life but I am here to challenge your thinking and your self talk. Can you think of a relationship that you feel is unhealthy or toxic to your being? Can you think of a relationship that leaves you feeling good about yourself and inspired? It's important to take note of those we surround ourselves by and more importantly how they make us feel on a daily basis. Why may you ask is this important? Because you are important, you are human and you deserve to be treated with dignity and respect. You deserve to be loved without conditions. So, if you can think of a relationship or two that leaves you contemplating who you are as a person, then maybe it's time to re-evaluate your circle. Maybe it's time to create some boundaries to protect your energy and your values.

Sometimes we try and hold on to certain relationships out of fear. This may be a fear of what life will look like without the individual, or it may be a fear of malicious acts that could arise if we cut ties with an individual or maybe it's a fear that if we cut the person off, we will never have a chance to rebuild a connection later in life with the same individual. At the end of the day, who are your go to people. Who is your ride or die person or persons? Who are the human beings that you go to in your worst moments and in your best, who celebrate you, who gently challenge you, who love you and who don't provide advice unless it's requested? You deserve to be surrounded by those people. The one's who uplift you and leave you feeling valued. The people who take a minute out of their busy day to listen intently and provide words of encouragement rather than provide you with solutions. Because I know it's not solutions you are looking for. You are looking to be heard by someone without judgement and to be understood.

You're going to cross paths with people who leave you feeling heavy, who steal a lot of your energy, who leave you feeling anxious and unsure about who you are and what you stand for. I say you're going too because I don't believe that we can get through life without these individuals. We need these individuals to cross our paths to remind us ever now and again of our worth. To remind us that we can come out stronger after struggle and hardship and to remind us that we need to stay true to ourselves and focus on our own journey. Seriously, if someone in your life can so easily throw you off your game, or make you second guess your choices in life, fuck, you are giving this person power. Take your damn power back and continue to be your authentic self. Do you know why I can say this with such confidence? Because I have experienced this. And the minute I created boundaries and took space in the relationship, is the minute I built my empire, followed by heart, my visions and said "I dare you to fuck with me". Now, don't get me wrong, I'm not a malicious person and I don't want to bring harm upon anyone. When I say I dare you to fuck with me, it really means say what you need to say to make yourself feel better, I'm going to allow your comment to enter into my left ear and leave my right ear, be the bigger person, smile and walk away. If you know SO strongly with all of your being what your purpose is, what you stand for and who you are, no one and I mean no one can bring you down or leave your questioning your worth or abilities.

Some of our relationships may seem like one-way streets. Maybe you feel as though you are always giving and never getting in return. Have you tried having a conversation with this person to let them know how you feel? Try it. They might not even recognize what they are doing or how it leaves you feeling. I've heard that communication can be quite an effective tool in relationships. I mean once you have had the conversation and the behaviour continues, then yes, maybe it's time to re-think the relationship and how it leaves you feeling. Some relationships are not worth the fight. The hardest part of ending a relationship or a contract with someone is accepting what will come with the loss of the relationship. Now I am not telling you to up and leave your spouse or end a relationship with a good friend; you need to put in the work and ask yourself the appropriate questions to determine if the individual is still right for you. You need to weigh the pros and cons of continuing with the relationship or ending it. Some people just aren't for you, and that's okay.

I challenge you to get real with yourself and dive into some heavy self-talk if you feel that a partner, a friend, a parent, a sibling, etc. are hurting, disrespecting you, undermining you or leave you feeling unsure of who you are. Then I challenge you to picture what ending your contract with that person would feel like, look like, sound like. Can you imagine yourself without this person in your life? If the answer is yes, do you feel peaceful? There is already enough chaos and drama in the world without added stress from people who are battling their own battles. Seriously ask yourself if this person is helping or hindering you from moving forward and attaining your goals in life. Only you can determine the signs of healthy versus unhealthy versus toxic. Your soul deserves love. Your soul deserves respect. Your soul deserves nourishment and acts of kindness. Of course, every relationship realistically comes with hardships, disagreements, and differences of opinions. I'm not encouraging you to walk away when things get a little tough, but I am encouraging you to look out for you and your well-being, this doesn't make you selfish. I don't want you to walk through life feeling undermined, abused, attacked, belittled, disrespected, or hurt over and over again. And please don't let people downplay your feelings by telling you, "Oh, but it's your cousin," or "Oh, but it's your sister." Family can be unhealthy too and just because there may be a blood relation does not mean that you have to continue a relationship if you feel it is unhealthy for you. Regardless of the relationship, you may have a deep love for one another but unfortunately, their ways of existing in the world might contradict yours. If this may be the case, then you may begin to feel resentment or bitterness toward the individual. If you're feeling more challenged than supported by an individual, and if you begin to question who you are and what you are striving toward in life because of things this individual might say, maybe it's time to break the contract for now and allow yourself to figure out if this person is helping or hindering your journey.

I'm sure most of us can think of someone who has taken a buttload of our energy from us through each interaction. The judgments and opinions of others can really leave you feeling overwhelmed, unsure of yourself, and frustrated. If you have ever felt manipulated, if you have ever felt like you have lost who you are while living in the same environment as someone, if you've tried to be a people-pleaser to gain their approval, or to anyone who has been in a physically, emotionally, spiritually, financially, or any type of abusive relationship, please tell yourself that you are worthy of moving on. I challenge you to look within yourself and review your own personal self-talk because usually the unhealthy relationships in your life are reflections of your inner feelings. Change your internal dialogue with yourself to self-empowerment, and you might be amazed with the results and your ability to remove toxicity from your life. You are worthy of peace; you are worthy of a beautiful life without added stress from individuals who are dealing with their own battles. Don't get me wrong; I'm not telling you to leave a relationship when there are struggles or challenges to overcome. I am simply saying that if you truly feel like a relationship drains more of your energy than it supports you, some re-evaluating might be useful. The bottom line is you don't have to put up with people's nonsense and people don't have to put up with yours. "You can't blame a clown for acting like a clown, you can only ask yourself why you keep going to the circus" – Dan Nielsen.

If you have a reoccurring issue or a power struggle with someone, you should check yourself first and foremost. Put your energy and attention into supporting you and changing your own perspective versus attempting to get someone who has hurt you to see what they have done. This conversation will be never-ending and will feel like a long-ass game of ping pong. You are not in the business of changing people; you simply do not have that power or ability. You do have the power and ability to focus on you. Focus on the things you can do to change or accept the situation you are in. Is your current situation or relationship making you feel angry? Maybe try forgiving the person and leaving the past in the past. This does not mean that you need to have an on-going relationship with this person, and it does not excuse what the person may have done to you, but it will allow you and your soul to move on peacefully without resentment. If there is someone in your life at this very moment that you are struggling to maintain a healthy relationship with, ask yourself this powerful question "what would you say to this person on their death bed". Some of the most beautiful healing can come from answering this question. No one is perfect. We are all on this earth trying to make it.

My nature and personality are very analytical. My genuine nature is to support people to become the best versions of themselves. Sometimes I can be overbearing and forceful with my efforts to support, but this only leaves people feeling attacked and on the defensive. I have learned to meet people where they are at, respect where they are at, and just allow it to be. So, if you are anything like me and you want the best for people but aren't sure how to provide support, just stop and listen. Allow the individual to do more of the talking; you'd be surprised how many people can create solutions to their problems by talking out loud and listening to themselves. Unless an individual wants to be helped, there's very little you can do for this person because they are not ready. And maybe you aren't the person who is meant to help them. I can only make the suggestion that sometimes backing away and providing space may support you in recognizing that you can't be a hero. Some people need to clear their baggage in and on their own time. Stop forcing the people in your relationships to change. This is not effective and will only leave the person feeling invalid. I will end this chapter with this quotation:

> Not all toxic people are cruel and uncaring. Some of them love us deeply. Many have good intentions. Most are toxic to our being because their needs and way of existing in the world force us to compromise ourselves and our happiness. They aren't inherently bad people, but they aren't the right people for us. And as hard as it is, we have to let them go. Life is hard enough without being around people who bring you down and as much as you care, you can't destroy yourself for the sake of someone else. You need to make your wellbeing a priority. Whether that means breaking up with

someone, loving a family member from a distance
or letting go of a friend. – Daniell Koepke

Relationships are hard. This chapter is just about letting you know that it is okay to walk away from an unhealthy situation. Sometimes something as simple as having physical space from a person can be the best thing for that relationship to flourish. "Boundaries can be a beautiful thing and if we have formally lived without them, it can be common to feel some guilt after we establish one. Sit in the discomfort of putting yourself first and start healing the people-pleasing behaviour you possess" – Mark Groves.

Lesson number three: Be ruthless with your boundaries and how you expend your energy. Respect yourself enough to stop tolerating the bullshit. "People will treat you differently when they sense that you have your own back" – Rachel Bell. People accept support on their own terms and at their own pace. You get to decide who stays in your life and who goes. Be kind and appreciate one another; life is too short for bullshit.

She Woke Up

Pain: Pain is an unpleasant feeling that is conveyed to the brain by sensory neurons. The discomfort signals actual or potential injury to the body. However, pain is more than a sensation, or the physical awareness of pain; it also includes perception, the subjective interpretation of the discomfort. Perception gives information on the pain's location, intensity, and something about its nature. The various conscious and unconscious responses to both sensation and perception, including the emotional response, add further definition to the overall concept of pain. — Urban Dictionary

Pain is an interesting thing. Some of us choose to endure pain for pleasure or to have something good come out of it, for example getting tattoos or undergoing labour and delivery. All of us experience pain in some form or another, whether that be physically or emotionally throughout our lifetime. So why do we often perceive pain as something negative, something unwanted, something to avoid? The reality is that none of us can get through life without pain, because if we didn't know what pain was or felt like, we would never appreciate pleasure. Without pleasure, we would never understand pain.

I find pain, like anger, to be a mask. It's easy to stay stuck in your pain, and it's tough as hell to get out or let go of your pain. Do you carry pain? The type of pain where you have pushed it soooooo far down into your being, to avoid, to bury, to forget? Trust me: it's easy to let the pain stay there, to dwell on it, to continue to relive it. The hard part is forgiving, sitting in your pain, allowing yourself to be vulnerable to experiencing pain and suffering all over again, and just letting the pain be. Burying this pain so far down can actually leave you feeling cold, bitter, and resentful, and the longer you let it brew, let it grow, the angrier you'll become. Have you ever felt so angry at someone that when you see their face, you just want to shoot a paintball at it? It's impossible to heal from something that has happened to us when we are angry and unwilling to forgive. The fact of the matter is no one will get any further ahead in life while suffering in their pain. Forgiveness and love can conquer all. Gratitude is a beautiful thing, but listen to me when I tell you: it is a long and fucking bumpy-ass road to get there. Being able to have love for those who have hurt us might seem impossible right now. This is because you are not ready to take the leap. You're not ready to say the most powerful, healing words known to mankind: "I forgive you and I have love for you." I'm not talking about the romantic, lustful kind of love; I'm talking about the unconditional kind of love.

Sometimes, you may believe that you're ready to heal, and so you will allow yourself to become vulnerable enough to let pieces of your pain surface. However, if you are not one hundred per cent ready and dedicated to the healing process, the universe will throw something at you with full force to see if you will retract and push the pain right back down the deep, dark hole. You will say, "Fuck no, this is too hard." You will say, "I was comfortable with how I was before." So, the question is, when do we ever know if we are ready to heal from our baggage? I don't have the answer for you. I'm sorry if you wanted me to be your voice of reason. You, my love, YOU possess all of the answers you need within you. Stop looking outward, and start looking inside your being.

So why, you might ask, is there pain and suffering in the world? Well, put simply, humans create it. As humans with every single emotion, we are bound to create hurt and upset in the world, to our loved ones, and to our so-called enemies. This past year, I have had people call me selfish. I have had people threaten me, guilt me, blame me, control me, hate me, and challenge me. I have also had people love me, respect me, support me, cherish me, lend me a helping hand, and provide me with a lesson. The reality is that YOU are not for everyone, and EVERYONE is not for you. So please, stop comparing yourself; stop trying to live to please those around you. You can live for yourself and still be kind; this doesn't make you selfish. You can live for yourself and still be giving. People will have their judgments. People will have their truths. <u>THEIR TRUTHS</u>. Their truths don't have to be your truths; you don't have to believe them.

If someone has hurt you, controlled you, blamed you, judged you, or criticized you, and if you feel as though your power and voice have been stripped from your being, maybe you need to take a good look at who is in your circle. You may need to do some cleansing, you may need to say goodbye to unhealthy relationships, and you may need to follow that intuition in your gut in order to live the life you so badly desire. It's going to take a lot of strength and a lot of courage to stand by your decisions. Only you know what is best and who is best for you. If someone has hurt you, maybe try not taking it personally. Instead, ask yourself, "What is going on for that person to say and do these hurtful things?" For example, the person who was bullied becomes the bully. Maybe that person who is hurting you has also had some deep hurt in their own life that they have yet to overcome. It's difficult in a moment of pain to think about why the pain has been inflicted. What is the actual act itself saying about the individual who is causing the pain? We all have layers of pain. Some are much deeper than others and, as Shrek and Donkey would say, "We are all onions and need to be peeled back one layer at a time." So, who are the people in your corner that will support you with peeling back your layers to free yourself of your pain?

I actually want to thank those who have challenged me by sharing their perspective and their opinions about me. I am human and I did once allow these opinions to bother me and to control me. I have learned that I am who I am and people can accept me or not. And I am okay with that. I want to challenge you to take this year to really look within your soul for your answers. I have learned that looking outwards for answers is an easier route. It's harder to look within; it's harder to find out who you truly are. I'm still on my path of figuring this out. Prayer, reiki, and therapy are all great tools to support you on your journey. But they are only tools. You possess all of your answers within. Listen to that intuition. Listen to that little voice in your head.

If you are saying yes to healing, then allow me to be a part of your journey. I am cheering you on from a distance. It's going to be extremely difficult. I promise that once you can get to a place where love fills your heart, and love is all you have to offer everyone, even those who have done harm to you, you will feel lighter. I believe in you. The journey of healing itself, although perceived as challenging, is one of the most beautiful things you can experience. Having an open heart allows for so much opportunity, so much love, and so much abundance in life. Are you going to continue to allow the opinions of others to run you? Are you going to believe the opinions of others to be true about yourself? Or are you strong enough to say, "I love myself enough to know that those are your truths, not mine." People are going to come on to your path to challenge you, to distract you from your bigger vision, and to slow you down. At the end of the day, blood relation or not, you get to decide who stays in your life and who goes. You don't have to be unkind to the individuals who judge you or challenge you. Just simply let them be. So, right now, I am giving you the voice that you believe you have lost. I'm lighting the fire under your ass to get moving in the direction of healing. I'm giving you the power that you feel you have relinquished. I am not God; I can't physically give you these things. But I believe in you so badly that I'm giving you permission to heal. If it is permission you are looking for, I'm granting that for you.

I know you are hurting. I know you might want revenge. I know you might want to prove something. I'm telling you right now that none of these feelings will get you ahead. They are in fact keeping you stuck in your pain. Forgiveness is everything. Try incorporating some of the following exercises into your daily life: 1. Look at yourself in the mirror every morning, and say the following affirmations: "I am enough," "I am worthy," "I am loved," "I am love and I spread it wherever I go," and "I love myself" as examples. Write them down as reminders in your phone; write notes to yourself and hide them around the house. Try this for a period of thirty days to see how you feel. It's a simple task that takes a minute out of your morning, noon, and night. 2. Write the name of the person who is challenging you or who hurt you on a piece of paper. Hang the paper on the bullseye of a dartboard and proceed to throw darts; however, I want you to purposefully miss the paper. Get your anger out, but don't actually hit the paper with the darts. I don't want you to cause harm to these individuals. Instead, I want you to release your pain and then forgive. Say aloud while you are throwing the darts everything that you forgive them for.

Lesson number four: If you're struggling, stop sitting in your pain. Stop remaining a victim of your circumstances. Change your situation instead of complaining about it. The ball is in your court. Life is not against you. Life itself is an opportunity. "There is always a solution, it might not be the one you want but there is one and it is attainable". – Eddie Pinero

Pregnancy

As mentioned in the previous chapter, there is pain that we choose to endure for something positive to come out of and there is pain that is inflicted without warning that is unwarranted. Pregnancy and birth were something I chose to endure for the sake of the reward at the end. I am not going to sugar-coat a damn thing in this chapter. There will be some gruesome content, so if you're a little twisted like me and enjoy hearing the gory details, you'll get a kick out of this chapter. Pregnancy is the time in a woman's life where commercials, social media, the internet, and books make it all seem like a breeze. Well, let me tell you my experience and the shit people don't talk about.

In January 2019, my incredible fiancé and I found out that we were pregnant. We had only been trying to conceive for a short time. I had been on birth control for ten straight years, so I am truly blessed for being one of the lucky mommas who was able to conceive and bear a child. I was grateful as I did not have morning sickness, and I did not get turned off of foods or smells. My fiancé and I were so excited to announce to family and friends that we would have a little bubs joining us in September of that year. Of course, in the beginning, it's all smiles and joy, but what you don't realize is how much you're about to lose yourself mentally, physically, and emotionally.

Sharing my body with this person inside of me was not my favourite. Some women absolutely love pregnancy and growing a human; I truly did not! In fact, I wish that my fiancé could bear our next one because I am dreading another pregnancy (don't get me wrong: it leads to the best thing life can give you, but I'm allowed to hate the process). Losing my figure was one of the hardest things that I had to accept during my pregnancy. This baby consumed me; I was literally growing a fucking human being with bones and brain cells and skin inside of me. I had not expected my body to change so quickly, but all I knew was that I began to hate myself, the way I looked, the way I felt, and the comments from other people. The worst part was I felt alone and like no one understood. I felt lost; I didn't feel like the Alysha that I knew. Of course, my fiancé would tell me, "You look beautiful," and "Don't say those things about yourself." Well thanks, honey, for trying to make me feel better, but until the baby is out, this is how I feel, and I need all the mommas to know that it is OKAY to feel that way. You are being validated by me. There is no code book of pregnancy, because it is different for each person. Your feelings are yours, so own them and don't feel ashamed by them. Oh, and also, if you care what people think about you, pregnancy is the time to literally stop fucking caring about anyone but yourself and that baby. People will literally spew shit out of their mouths to "compliment you," to "comment on your changing body," and to "give you advice about your unborn child." I wasn't having any of it. What people need to realize is that being pregnant does not give them automatic permission to comment on your body or give advice without being asked. Pregnancy does not give them permission to touch my belly without asking. Yes, I am a hugger with close family and friends, but if I am not close to you or I do not know you, do not fucking touch me and leave your comments in your brain, thanks.

The worst and hardest is when family comment on your changing body. Thank you for noticing that my hips have gotten wider; thank you for noticing that I am swollen and carrying a lot of water weight. It blows my mind because it's as if people forget that mirrors exist. AGAIN, I am growing a human inside of my body, so yes, I am aware that my feet look like Shrek's, and I am aware that my hips are wider, because if you didn't already know, I am pushing a baby out of my vagina (my hips are making room to do so). I think I became a little bitter in my pregnancy and it hasn't worn off yet ☺. My point is don't be afraid to nicely or not nicely tell people how you feel and for people to back off. Pregnancy already leaves you on the biggest emotional roller coaster ride known to the human race, so us mommas don't need the extra babble that shoots out of people's mouths. Stand your ground, Momma, you will get through it.

Let's fast forward to the third trimester. At times I thought that I was bearing a knife as opposed to a baby inside of me because of the brutal, stabbing pains in my left rib. I could not get comfortable sleeping; my back hurt like a bitch. They tell you not to sleep on your back because it can put pressure on the baby; well, screw you, internet; I'll sleep on my damn back if I want to if it ensures I'll be "comfortable." I used up all three hundred dollars of my benefits in like two fucking sessions at the chiropractor's. Not to mention I was also going to regular prenatal massages and therapy for my mental health. Needless to say, I was breaking the bank before the baby even arrived to try and take care of myself. Speaking of taking care of yourself, let's talk about the courses that your doctor suggests for you to attend to prepare you for this baby. Let's just be honest with ourselves: it doesn't matter how many books you read, courses you take, or experts you talk to: you will never feel one hundred per cent prepared for the arrival of your baby. Half of the time I find myself making shit up as I go. I don't know what the fuck I'm doing on a daily basis as a mom, but I'm keeping her alive, healthy, and I think happy (she smiles at me a lot).

Back to the courses that are heavily forced upon you to take by medical professionals: there's a breastfeeding course, a postpartum course, and a labour and delivery course. I somehow made it through the breastfeeding course, and I must say that I did learn a lot, although I was feeling extremely anxious about breastfeeding. Just the thought of a little baby relying on me and my body to feed them left me feeling uneasy (I will get into more detail in the next chapter). I attended thirty minutes of the postpartum course and then, out of the blue, I began to feel lightheaded, sweaty, and nauseous. I left the room and found myself having the biggest panic attack of my life, and to this day, I am unsure of what triggered it. I went for some fresh air; that didn't help. I ate a granola bar; that didn't seem to help. I sat down and closed my eyes; that didn't help. The only thing that I could think of doing was attempting to get inside my own head to calm myself down. I told myself over and over that this wasn't good for my baby, and I used deep breathing to relax myself. Finally, after twenty minutes, I gained my sight again and gathered the strength to speak with the instructor. I decided right then and there that I didn't need these damn courses to prepare me to raise my child. There is nothing wrong with the courses, they are certainly packed with information, but being the free-spirited soul that I am, the courses weren't for me. So I ditched the eight-hour labour and delivery course that took place on a Saturday and instead spent time with my significant other because I had come to realize that time is precious and that we weren't going to have the luxury of waking up on a Saturday to do what we wanted when this baby arrived. I believe we went to the market as this was something that we loved doing together on a Saturday to purchase fresh fruit and wood decor for the house.

After this panic attacked occurred, I really got to thinking that I needed to put myself and this baby first. I decided to take mat leave one month early (now I am thankful, because I live in Canada and I get to have one year off). By week thirty-six of my pregnancy, I had stopped wearing a bra to work because I couldn't stand the pressure it put on my ribs. I wore flowy dresses that I bought from a clothing store called International Clothing for a cheap-ass price because fuck, the maternity stores really know how to break a bank account. I am already a sweaty person to begin with, so pregnancy of course just emphasized that piece even more. The flowy dresses helped to get a breeze up in the old whoha once in a while. To say the least, I was ready for this little fucker (I mean angel) to exit my body. I was trying to give her an early eviction notice, but since she is a Virgo, she is a little stubborn. One more thing before I get on to the gruesomeness: SEX was nonexistent, or at least it was for me. Sex hurt: it was not enjoyable by the end of my pregnancy; it was more like a chore. I felt bad for my lover, leaving him deprived, but sex was taken off the table for a few months.

Okay, you twisted people, here is my labour and delivery experience. First off, I love to meditate, and through my meditation I use crystals and I talk to people who have passed over, in this case, by my aunt's father, Peter (who was like a father to me), and my dad's father, Bob. I am a very intuitive person; some people think I am batshit crazy, but c'est la vie. I had a feeling throughout my entire pregnancy that my baby would make her arrival on September 14th, 2019 and she did just that. I straight-up asked Peter in one of my meditations when my baby would arrive, and he told me my water would break at 9:30 p.m. on September 13th and that she would be born on the 14th. I was so sure that my baby was coming on this date that I told my family, my fiancé's family, and my friends, and I don't quite think that many believed me. I even told my doctor that he would have to work on Saturday, September 14th and that he shouldn't make any plans because this baby was coming. He laughed and said, "I will book the whole day for you."

So, come September 13th, I was nesting like crazyyyyy, the house was spotless, and I went for three walks; I was determined for my missy to arrive. My fiancé and I fell asleep at 9 p.m. on the 13th and liquid started gushing, I mean gushing out of me, at 10 p.m. on the 13th. I rolled over and said, "Babe, my water broke." He thought I was joking until he witnessed the amount of liquid that came out of me and on to the sheets and bathroom floor. I sat on the toilet for a good five minutes while this liquid continued to gush out of my body. I put on a giant maxi pad and an old pair of pants and we hit the road. My fiancé texted his family to which they thought we were pulling a prank on them because I was bang-on about the date of baby's arrival. I called and texted my family and the journey began. We arrived at the hospital, checked in, and were admitted quickly. The nurse monitored my contractions and told me I was three centimetres dilated. The nurse then asked to see my pad, to which she revealed to us that our little missy had taken a huge shit in utero when my water broke. This meant that she could potentially ingest her shit and I needed to be monitored throughout my labour. (Things no one prepares you for. I had no fucking idea what this meant until it actually happened to me and my babe.)

We got comfy and settled in our room which had beautiful big windows and a shower; it felt comfortable. I pulled out my phone and my headphones and listened to my rap playlist I had made throughout my pregnancy. My fiancé tried to take a catnap as he had just worked a long-ass day, and at this point, I was just chilling out and not in pain. I played Post Malone's "Rockstar" on repeat which got me through my tougher contractions. With my crystal in one hand and my beats in the other, I was determined more than ever to get this baby out. The nurse checked me at 2 a.m. and told me I was in active labour and five centimetres dilated. The pain was averaging around a four out of ten at this point, and I was managing the contractions. Before I knew it, the contractions came on so strong and so fast, I didn't know what hit me. With each contraction my famous words were, "Fuck, fuck, fuck." I could feel my magnificent fiancé's hand stroking my back and sitting in my pain with me. I could hear the nurses telling me, "You got this, girl." The nurse suggested I take a shower and put some heat on my back. So, into the shower I go with the love of my life to follow. He held the shower head over my back and body which felt amazing. And at this very moment I instantly stopped giving a shit about what I looked like, smelled like, or what was going to come out of my body when I began pushing. I accepted the fact that I would not be "Instagram glamorous" when baby girl arrived for our first photo.

Out of the shower I came and my contractions became unbearable. My fiancé asked the nurse if I could get an epidural as I was passing in and out, white as a ghost, and all I could hear was, "Alysha, stay with us." The nurse checked once again and told me that I was ten centimetres dilated (which to anyone delivering their first baby means fully fucking dilated). I had made it all the way to ten centimetres without an epidural; I felt like Superwoman. You better bet your ass I got that epidural, and real quick. I was poked and pried in my veins to get the IV in, jabbed in the spine for the epidural, a catheter was shoved up my pee hole, and all I could think was, "Oh, Alysha, please don't get a bladder infection from this." The nurse told me that we were going to do a few practice pushes before the doctor arrived. After two pushes, the nurse told me to stop pushing as she could see the baby's head. She then told me that I needed to basically hold the baby in and stop pushing until the doctor arrived. My doctor lived five minutes from the hospital and those five minutes felt like an eternity. My doctor finally arrived and I joked with him and said, "I told you that you would have to work today," to which he joked that he had his calendar cleared just for me on that day.

We got right down to business, and with five pushes our little missy was born. Now here is where shit got real, I mean literal shit. The doctors placed my baby on my chest and both her and I were covered in baby shit. I'm telling you the first poop from a baby is pure tar, like call Mr. Clean up in this bitch to help scrub you off because damn, that's a lot of poop. The nurse commented, "I have never seen anything like this in my life." And in my head I'm like, glad I can fucking amuse you; maybe it should go into *The Guinness Book of World Records*? Then the emotions kicked into overdrive and I cried, and while I was holding this precious bean, the doctors all gave me a spiel. My doctor told me that I almost had a buttgina (vagina butt) because Little Missy gave me a third-degree tear. Yes, there are four degrees of tears that you can receive with a vaginal birth. So, the plastic surgeon came in and stitched me up, told me I needed to take RestoraLAX daily for six weeks because I could not have a solid bowel movement (for fear of tearing the stitches). The doctor also told me that I would go home and basically be an emotional wreck who would cry for no reason, and he told me the most important thing of all: "Reach out and ask for help if you are struggling with your emotions." Listen to me, Mommas: do not sit and struggle with your emotions or hormones pre- or post-birth. Those hormones are out of your control whether you like it or not, and only they will decide when it's time to regulate again. ASK FOR HELP if you are struggling in the slightest, because you are not alone.

I want to take this opportunity to thank the labour and delivery nurses of the world, and I am advocating that you all get a raise because, shit, you do all of the work (sorry, Doc; it's true). The doctor basically comes into the room last minute to catch the baby from falling on to the floor. All the prep work, guidance, and support are from the nurses. Giving birth is not, I repeat is not, how you view it in movies. So, thank you labour and delivery nurses for your expertise, and goddammit, government, give them a raise.

Lesson number five: You'll find your own groove, Momma; GIVE yourself more credit!!!! Whatever experiences you encounter during your pregnancy and delivery, they are your experiences, so own them and don't be afraid to ask for support.

Holy Shit, I am a Mom

I was fucking starving after giving birth. I even packed snacks for myself to eat at the hospital before (which I highly recommend), but I was seriously starving from using my energy to get this beautiful creature out of my body. Luckily, our babe was born at 5:44 a.m. and so breakfast was on its way. The nurse and my fiancé helped me out of bed to use the washroom to ensure that my legs were working again from the epidural. WARNING: Do not look down at the ground after you give birth, because it will look like *The Texas Chainsaw Massacre* movie on the floor.

If you are one of the lucky moms to receive the lovely gift of a third-degree tear or higher, you will hate your life for the next two weeks or more and that's just fact. You can forget the toilet paper for the next month or so. You cannot take a piss or a shit without a squeeze bottle in one hand and a mirror in the other. YES, you need to look at the destruction of your female anatomy daily to ensure that nothing gets infected! You will need to squeeze warm water on your lady bits and anus for cleansing after each bathroom use. I also strongly recommend that you purchase a perineal spray that contains witch hazel (you will feel instant relief). The internet tells you to purchase maxi pads prior to giving birth. I say fuck the maxi pads and go to Costco to buy the huge pack of Depends diapers. This can be the first thing that you and your baby have in common… wearing a diaper. The reason I say choose the diaper is because you will bleed and bleed and bleed for up to six weeks. Luckily, my bleeding only lasted three weeks, but those diapers saved a lot of bed sheet washing.

Remember how I told you at the beginning that I was going to be brutally honest in this book? Well, this is me sharing my feelings about breastfeeding. I am that person who sees a woman in public and judges them for exposing their breasts and not covering up. I am that person who sees that same woman and assumes she's doing this to seek attention and show off her huge milk-filled breasts to all of the males of the world who might be bored of looking at their wives' boobs. I am probably one of the few who doesn't think milk coming out of a human breast is natural. I just couldn't comprehend how your partner could go from pleasuring you with those breasts of yours to a baby sucking on them for food. Of course, I have sexualized boobs, and so the information above that I share with you makes sense in my brain; it doesn't have to make sense to you.

With all of that said, I listened to the doctors and the books and the internet, I challenged my perceptions, and I gave breastfeeding a shot. It was as terrible as I expected it to be. My baby basically ripped off my left nipple and left it bloody and raw. My baby had a good suck on her; she was my strong little gal, and man, did she get her sense of determination from her momma. She wanted that liquid gold, and bad. Luckily, one of the nurses worked with me to try and get her to latch, but with each attempt, my baby wouldn't latch properly and lacked the patience to get milk out of her momma. Momma just wasn't producing. The hospital gave me a breast pump, to which nothing came out. The nurses asked if I wanted a bottle of formula, and I said very happily, "Yes please." I fed my baby ten millilitres of formula which filled her little marble-sized belly and she was out like a light.

My doctor came to check us out the next day while still in the hospital. He asked me how feeding was going, and I honestly said that I was struggling with breastfeeding. He told me not to put all of my eggs into the breastfeeding basket and that fed babies are healthy babies, doesn't matter how they were fed. He gave me the name of a lactation consultant to seek support from if I chose to do so. I felt a sense of relief in this moment, and for the next three weeks, I used a mixture of pumped breast milk and formula. My baby was 7'10 when she was born and she was a whopping 8'2 the week after she was born!! This made me feel like a champion as a new mother, because it meant my baby was growing and that she was healthy. I just want to mention that I am a reserved person with my body, but I didn't give a rat's ass who saw my boobs if it meant feeding my baby. I basically could have considered myself to be a pornographic superstar with the number of nurses that were grabbing and looking at my boobs.

We set off on our journey back home as new parents, not knowing what the fuck we were doing and basically pretending like we did. I couldn't sit for a good week and a half because of my stitches. Let me tell you, trying to breastfeed while standing does not work. I used pillows and blankets to prop her up enough for me to lean over, apply the nipple shield, and feed her. My back was absolutely fucked. So, on top of my ripped-open vagina and my bloody breasts, I now had an aching back to which I just accepted that it would continue to ache for the next five years of my life at least.

One beautiful Sunday morning, my lover was outside cutting the grass, and I was upstairs attempting to breastfeed the baby. After ten minutes of attempting to properly latch her on the nipple shield while propped up on pillows, I thought to myself, "I need to shit. My man is outside, and I'm here by myself, and I need to shit." So, the only logical thing I could think of was, "Okay, Alysha, you are wearing a diaper; just shit in the diaper like your baby." I did just that. See the thing is, I laughed my ass off while this was happening because after you give birth to a child, your body does what it wants, ladies, and you can't stop it. Every sneeze comes with a drizzle in the undies; get used to it! I knew in that moment that I had reached my peak of not giving a fuck. From this point forward, nothing could faze me because I had basically lost all dignity and I wasn't about to put up with anyone's bullshit.

Sleep deprivation is a real thing. I didn't sleep for a total of like sixty hours by the time we got home from the hospital. I was so sleep-deprived that my brain would not allow me to fall asleep but instead wondered how the next twenty years would be raising a child: what if my baby got sick, what if I got frustrated and took my emotions out on the baby, what if, what if. I tried listening to music, counting backwards from one hundred, meditating, and deep breathing. It actually got to the point where I was going to take myself to the hospital because I could feel my heart beating right out of my chest (I seriously thought I might have a heart attack at the age of twenty-six) due to lack of sleep. Finally, I got to sleep for a couple of hours; I think my body just knew that if I didn't, I would die. I became the master of functioning off of broken sleep: two hours here, two hours there, yet somehow feeling pretty rejuvenated in the morning. Mind you, the only way I was getting this sleep is if Little Missy was in the bed beside her momma.

Right off the bat, Little Missy hated her bassinet. She hated laying straight on her back; she was kind of a queen. Being a sleep-deprived momma, I would have done anything for those two hours of sleep, so my fiancé claimed the spare bedroom and I claimed our bed with the babe. ALL of the books and internet will tell you "do not co-sleep, blah, blah blah." Honestly, Momma, you need to do what's best for you and your baby. I never imagined that our baby would kick her daddy out and move into our bed, but it happened. I hated it because it meant a broken back for me, it meant sleeping with one eye open, it meant losing an important piece of my relationship with my fiancé. By week five, I was pretty sick of having the baby in the bed beside me but I didn't know how to transition her. Then I began putting her down in her crib during the day for naps. I needed her to learn how to self-soothe, and I needed her to learn that she was safe without being held 24/7. I also want to mention that the minute you push that baby out, it's like God hands you a set of skills you never knew you had. I'm telling you they just magically appear out of thin air. It makes you feel somewhat warm inside knowing "you got this." From a fellow momma, I need you to know that you got this, and you will make it through those hard nights, those cries, those messy diapers.

Being a mom is the hardest job on the planet; well, at least for me it is. I could work with people with addiction issues, people mental health issues, and people who have murdered with no problem, but being a mom, that's tough shit. There are days where I absolutely love being a mom and a parent to that little angel, and then there are days when I absolutely hate every minute of it. I need you to know that this is okay. It is okay to have good days and bad days. I need to make one thing clear: on my bad days I do not love my child any less, I love her unconditionally, but some days I want to scream. I made one promise to myself and that was to never take any of my emotions or anger out on my baby. So, at times, I would place her in her swing and walk away for a few minutes to punch a pillow or cry. I always compose myself to come back and give my baby all the love she deserve but I need some sort of release in those moments of feeling weak, helpless, and frustrated. Our missy is such a content baby, too, so I was honest with myself and the people around me and told people that if she had been a colicky baby, I would be fearful of developing postpartum depression. I know myself well enough to know what my patience can and cannot tolerate. I am letting all you parents know that parenting is harder than hard. It will push you to limits you never knew were possible.

With my broken sleep patterns, staying at home with a baby all day every day, and not having many interactions, I didn't have much to say. I felt myself becoming bitter, resentful, impatient, irritable, and rude to my partner. I understood that the reality was that he needed to go to work to bring in an income for the family, but I resented the fact that he could go interact with other human beings. I resented him for not being able to be home with me 24/7 with this baby. I resented that we needed to sleep in separate rooms because of a baby. The reality was I missed the convenience of life before a baby, and it was really hard to adjust to sacrificing time, money, and relationships for this same baby. Like, all of my time was consumed by this little person who relied so heavily on me. It was all too much at times. I am telling you that a baby will test your relationship with your lover. So, if you can make it through those tough times and still come out loving one another, then you can make it through anything.

On top of feeling all of the emotions listed in the previous paragraph, there is colicky crying added into the mix. I am a very self-aware individual; therefore, I know my limit. I know when my patience has been pushed to that limit. A crying, colicky baby absolutely pushes me to my wits' end. I know that if I cannot calm my baby within thirty minutes, then I am walking away because I need a break. I am going to be completely honest. In my moments of weakness, I have said these things out loud with my partner in the room: "This is fucking ridiculous," "I don't care what you do with her, I need to leave," and "Holy fuck." Of course, the guilt kicks in afterwards when I have calmed and collected myself, and then I feel absolutely terrible for swearing or blaming the baby when she's screaming her head off for no apparent reason. I know my baby's cries. There is her pain cry, which I only hear when she is getting a needle; there is her hungry cry; and then there is her colic "I don't know why the fuck I'm crying" cry. It has taken a lot of trial and error, but I have finally figured out that I can usually place her tummy tight against mine and put a soother in her mouth while walking and bouncing the halls, and then she's usually settled and out like a light in thirty minutes. When this doesn't work, and the screaming persists, my fiancé and I give her a dropper of Infacol which seems to calm her almost instantly. My fiancé found Infacol at the local pharmacy, and I am seriously so thankful that he did. That shit is magic. (I am not a doctor, so I am not recommending this to anyone. Talk to your doctor first.) I really try not to make a habit of giving it to her unless she has been screaming bloody murder for two or more hours. I just don't want her little body to depend on it for comfort. So, I know myself enough to admit that colic and crying are my triggers. I don't possess the patience within to stay focused on calming a baby without becoming angry. It's normal to feel this way, by the way. Again, it's not a bad thing; you just need to know when to ask for help and the suggestions that come with the help.

Listen to me when I tell you to accept help when it's offered. I struggle to accept help from anyone because I am very stubborn and independent, but when you have a baby, you are tested all the time and you need to make time for yourself. I was so blessed to have the support from my mother-in-law, my fiancé's family, and my friends, along with the emotional support from my family provinces away. The first two weeks after you bring that baby home, you will struggle to separate from them. I thought that I knew my baby best and cared for my baby best, and so it challenged me when other people would take her and care for her. I am not afraid to admit that I became defensive at times. I would take the baby out of people's arms to try and soothe her myself; I would comment on the way my partner would hold our baby. I thought that I knew best. How could I not; I'm the mother! Boy, how wrong I was. But I needed to learn that my baby would be okay without me, without my presence. Once I realized this, then I was able to fall asleep, even if she began to cry, knowing that she was in good hands. Trust me, when you are the one home with your baby 24/7, you feel superior to everyone else, you feel like you know best, and you kind of become a bitch, a know-it-all. But when you can come to the realization that you are not the be-all and end-all and that this baby needs other relationships to thrive in life, then you can start to relax knowing that your baby will be safe with Grandma, safe with Dad, and safe with friends who are only trying to support you and allow you to get some rest.

Make time for date nights with your partner on a monthly basis if you have a family member or a baby sitting on speed dial. I can't stress enough how important time is with your partner after the baby comes. You will feel as though your world centres around this baby. I challenge you to fit the baby into your current lifestyle as opposed to changing your lifestyle because of the baby. So, if you and your partner go to Costco for groceries every Saturday, then I don't suggest you stop because you had a baby. You need this alone time together to appreciate one another, to support one another, and to reconnect on a new level. Parenting is full of trial and error, and you will feel frustrated at some points. Make sure you tell your partner that they matter, and give words of encouragement. Do what you need to do to take care of yourself and your partner. Mommy and Daddy, you are the key players in this little babe's world, so take care of one another, and don't go a single day without telling your partner that you love and appreciate them.

So, New Momma or Seasoned Momma, I need you to hear this: you are fucking amazing. You are doing the absolute best that you know how. Give yourself more credit, because without you, that little miracle would not be here. You are a rock star. You are a superhero. You are the Incredible Hulk. You are a mom, a great fucking mom! Find little moments of inspiration throughout the day that keep you going. Join mom groups; join mommy and baby fitness classes. Babies are going to cry in public, in the car seat, and on the airplane, but it shouldn't stop you from travelling or getting out of the house. Do what you need to do to not only survive but enjoy parenthood, and for God's sake, ask for help.

It's the little moments that keep me going. The smiles from my little bean make my heart melt and let me know that I am doing a good job. So as much as being a mom is hard, and although there are days that you hate motherhood, that baby needs you. That baby needs their momma to be the best version of themselves. My daughter is the best thing that has ever happened to me in my life. Love turns to a whole new level when you bring a child into the world.

To my baby girl: when you are old enough to read this, Mommy needs you to know that you are special, you are one of a kind, you are you, you are loved, you are worthy, you are beautiful inside and out, and you have the world at your fingertips. Don't ever let anyone tell you that you can't do something. Don't ever let anyone tell you to settle. Don't ever let anyone tell you that you are not good enough. I believe in you, my girl, and I love you to the mountain peaks and back a million times.

Lesson number six: Make time for yourself, Momma! This is a must, because a healthy momma will be able to care for her family. Your baby needs you to be healthy mentally and physically, because that little bean is counting on you. Wake up every morning, look in the mirror, and say, "I am a great fucking mom and I've got this." Snuggle and love them up while you can, because before you know it, they'll be out the door conquering this world.

The good old postpartum depression. I wasn't going to write about this because I believed with all of my heart that I didn't struggle with it. Well, I was wrong. I kept telling myself that I was fine, but my actions were telling me otherwise. It wasn't until my little missy had turned three months old that I recognized I was struggling. I wish I could tell you how I figured it out but I seriously think I just woke up one day and gave myself permission to struggle with motherhood. My brain said, "Alysha, you're fine; you don't struggle with PPD," but my thoughts and actions sure as fuck confirmed that I did. Did you know that in my mom group the registered nurse told us that ninety per cent of moms struggle with PPD? Ninety fucking per cent. That's a lot of struggling mommas out there. Why in God's name aren't we supporting one another? Let's use the village to raise these kiddos! We don't need to be superhumans raising them on our own.

Get involved in the community! The best thing you can do if you are struggling is get involved and let it be known that you are struggling. Don't feel afraid or embarrassed to talk about your thoughts, actions, behaviours, and perceptions about motherhood. Join parent groups at your local library or health unit. Join a mommy and baby swim class or a fit mommy program at your local gym. Or if you are like me and want to save money, go for walks with other moms, go to the dog park, and have moms over for tea and a good chat. The best decision I ever made was joining a six-week mommy and baby program where I had the privilege of meeting and getting to know fifteen other mommas and babes. We still meet bi-weekly in the community or rotate hosting at our homes to do arts and crafts with our babes and let our babes socialize with one another. If you are struggling and someone offers help, take it!!!!! I can't say that any clearer. Take help when it is offered and don't be afraid to ask if you need a break. I remember one day in particular when my little missy wouldn't settle all day. I felt fits of rage come over me. I yelled at the fucking spaghetti squash I was making for dinner because it wasn't cooking fast enough… I yelled at a fucking vegetable. A friend who I had met in my group sent me a message to check in and, in that moment, I felt at ease knowing that someone was in my corner. She reminded me that I could not pour from an empty cup and that's when I told myself that I needed a break. So, I messaged my partner and told him that when he got home from work, he needed to take the baby so I could have some me time. I took a bath, listened to my motivational podcasts, wrote my gratitude list, and felt a little better. I am just so thankful to have people in my corner when I need them: people who don't judge me, and people who say they will be there for me any time of day and they mean it. Motherhood is intense, so please don't do it alone.

I am self-aware enough to know that I had become bitter, impatient, resentful, insensitive, bitchy, irrational, and downright mean. I'd tell the dog to fuck off on a daily basis because he walked behind me and basically tripped me and the baby. Alysha, he is just a dog being a dog, doing the same dog things as he did before the baby came. I convinced myself that my relationship with my partner sucked and that we had lost all connection. I was impatient as fuck and short-tempered. I ate like shit. Some days I basically woke up and said fuck all of this; I love my family, but fuck this. Some days I wanted to just leave and take a weekend vacation without my phone or civilization. The brutal and honest truth is I miss my life before a baby. I am dealing with PPD because I am grieving the loss of my past freedom, time, money spent on things for me, my hot body, eight-hour sleeps every night, my dignity, and my past connection with my partner. I am grieving and I am not dealing with it correctly. I have lied to myself so well that I have talked myself out of accepting that I struggle with PPD. It doesn't help that everyone around me says, "Oh wow, you have such a good baby." If I try to vent to people about my frustrations or my emotions, I get, "But truly, you have it pretty good." My thoughts, feelings, and emotions get downplayed by people because "You have a good baby."

What the fuck is the definition of a good baby? See, my bitterness is coming through strongly because this is a huge trigger for me. I don't mean to offend the people who say this because deep down I know that this comment is being made to support me and make me feel good. This is just a good reminder that I am struggling. I guess having a good baby means that they don't cry all of the time? If this is the case then yes, I do have a pretty good baby BUT I'm struggling with my emotions, motherhood and grief regardless of having a "good or bad" baby. I need people to hear that it is OKAY to feel this way. I got so used to people telling me that I am doing a good job with my baby that I have allowed it to mask what's really going on underneath it all. Underneath it all, I want to scream. I swear like a mother trucker (I mean, I always swore, but it's become a little extra). I so badly didn't want to be a part of the ninety per cent statistic of moms who struggle with postpartum depression, but I am and it's okay. Every mom is a rock star regardless if you're struggling or not. Every mother deserves to be heard and validated. So, my question to myself is what am I going to do about it? Because my message to my readers throughout my book is to accept help when struggling, don't sit and dwell in your pain, and find a way to work through it, I am giving myself permission to seek support.

I am making a promise to myself to attend a weekly postpartum depression support group and therapy at least once per month. It is OKAY to not be okay. I just pushed a living, breathing human out of my vagina, so yes, it is okay for me to struggle with my emotions, my relationships, and my life. Postpartum depression doesn't have to include thoughts of suicide or thoughts of harming the baby. I haven't had any dark thoughts of self-harm or harm to my baby, but I have become very impatient. I do swear and say things like, "This is fucking ridiculous," "I don't care what you do with the baby; I'm going upstairs," and "This dog is fucking annoying." I need to step back and check in with myself. Listen here, Momma, you are allowed to struggle. This process is crazy, it's challenging, it's frustrating, it's all insane. But you and your mental health matter. You are the one home with this little person for a year (if you live in Canada). You need to make sure that you feel healthy mentally, emotionally, and physically. If you start taking things out on the dog, or on your partner, or on the in-laws, then I challenge you to ask yourself if you're struggling. If you feel as though you are more irritable and more on edge, if you get pissed off at little things like not having the type of cereal you like in the house, then check in with yourself. I had a million acquaintances give me information for PPD support groups. I thought nothing of it; in fact, I thought it was kind of random until one morning I woke up and said, "These people who barely know me recognize that I am clearly struggling with PPD. The universe is telling these people to reach out to me. I just need to pay attention and listen to the messages."

I really don't like the term "postpartum depression." I think I am going to call it postpartum reality. You don't have to feel depressed to be struggling. You don't have to have thoughts of harming the baby to be struggling. I don't like adding a label into the mix. I think it is pretty normal for every mother to feel challenged, sad, frustrated, etc. after having a baby. The hormones definitely play a part in this. You really don't know how you will act or feel until the baby is physically present in your arms 24/7. To be honest, I can't wait for my baby to grow up and be able to communicate her needs with me, because trying to figure out her cries and her needs as a baby is fucking crazy. I am not a fucking mind reader, so it would be great if someone could invent something to communicate with babies (hint hint, if someone wants to get filthy rich).

It took me three months to figure out that I was actually struggling with my emotions and the adjustment of having a baby. I did an extremely good job of denying it and hiding it from others. I literally woke up one day and said, "Alysha, you are struggling more than you're allowing yourself to believe, and it's not healthy." My first group therapy session I attended really opened my eyes to how much I was struggling. I instantly started crying like a baby when I told the group my thoughts and feelings about motherhood, that MY expectations of my partner weren't being followed, and that I didn't sign up to feel like a single mom. I really don't want to make it sound like my partner does nothing, because he is a fabulous human being. He is excellent at cleaning the house, making dinners, going to work to provide for the family, and making our baby laugh and feel loved. But I felt as though I was doing all of the "mundane tasks" for our baby like bathing and diaper-changing and soothing and feeding, and it all became too much; this is where the resentment kicked in. I realized that I had allowed my partner to become comfortable as I accepted all of the "hard work" and responsibility, and I didn't give him a chance to explore these for himself. I don't think he recognized how challenging it was on a daily basis caring for our child, and I seriously didn't take his feelings or thoughts into consideration, either. I also didn't take into account how difficult it was for him to go to work every single day, work his ass off, and then come home to help take care of a brand-new little baby. That must have been tough as fuck. So, for all the dads out there who are just doing the best that they can and the best that they know how, I thank you and I appreciate you.

I was feeling so down and so desperate for an escape that I seriously thought about leaving for a weekend and giving myself a break from it all to venture to the mountains. I was having fantasies of escaping from my family's presence. I craved a break so badly that I was willing to go somewhere with minimal to no cell reception and be completely isolated because this was what I thought was going to help me. The truth is that motherhood is fucking hard, and I wanted to run some days, but I quickly realized that running away wouldn't solve anything. It might give me ease for a brief moment, but it was not going to magically solve my problems, my fears, or my frustrations. So, I am giving future Alysha permission to go on my mountain adventure alone, but only when Alysha is in a good headspace, and not for the purpose of avoiding or running from her problems, but simply to get out and enjoy the beauty of nature and have some self-care. I don't think couples actually realize the challenges that come with having a child. These are my feelings and my truths. They might or might not relate to you.

Let's just get deep for a moment here. Relationships have their good days and bad days; we all know that. Some days you want to laugh and love deeply, and other days you want to fucking rip each other's hair out. It is so damn important to take space in your relationship. Go out with your girlfriends, go for a walk, or go to the gym alone. Build a life outside of this person for your own sanity and well-being. I'm asking you to be more self-aware and a little selfish sometimes to take care of you and your needs, especially when you are caring for a baby 24/7. If you need a trip to Vegas, talk to your partner and find a way to take the trip to Vegas. You had lives before one another, and that shouldn't stop because you entered into a romantic relationship or had a child. You'll drive each other crazy if you are together one hundred per cent of the time. I'm sure by now that you already know what pushes your buttons to the limit. If not, pay attention, because it can make you extremely resentful if you allow it to affect you. I became resentful about simple tasks not being done by my partner such as cleaning the bottles. And the thing is, it was my issue. I didn't communicate what I needed from my partner and I had an expectation in my head that he would just know to clean the bottles. Communicate your needs because people aren't mind readers and people will do tasks differently than you do. Let it be.

Since having a baby, I have noticed a shift in our relationship. I wouldn't say that this shift is for the worse, but it's definitely been an eye-opening experience. Lack of sleep, postpartum depression, and a lifestyle change has definitely made me become less patient, more unrealistic with my expectations, shorter-tempered, and kind of a bitch in general. To be honest, my relationship with my fiancé is the last thing on my mind throughout the day because I have been focusing all of my attention on the baby, making dinner, going to mom groups, walking the dog, and trying to catch up on sleep while attempting to maintain my sanity. As I sit here and write this, I realize I am bitter as fuck. This I-don't-give-a-fuck kind of attitude seems to be creeping into my romantic relationship, and I'm not okay with this. What do to, what to do? (Alysha's inner voice says…) "Book a fucking therapy session, dumbass; you clearly need to vent." I swear therapy is the secret to life. You can vent all of your most fucked-up feelings, emotions, and thoughts out loud to a complete stranger and they aren't allowed to tell anyone unless you threaten to hurt someone or yourself. So, some day you will struggle and some days you will feel great and tell yourself you got this. I will remind you, YOU GOT THIS! Communicate your needs and check in with yourself often.

I guess I just want to remind people to think before you speak. Unsolicited advice is a trigger to new parents. As a new parent, I am trying to figure things out on and in my own way. I know you were once a mother or a father as well and you have been through the ringer once or twice but it doesn't mean you can give your advice on demand. I know it's only natural for people to try and jump in to offer advice to make things easier on you, but I'm asking you not too provide it unless I ask for it. There are so many different ways to change a diaper or to put on the baby's onesie. There are so many different ways to introduce solid foods or to potty train. There is no right way to parent. So please, just think before you offer your advice to a new parent.

Lesson number seven: It's okay to not be okay. Take it one day at a time. Get involved in the community and remember to take time to care for yourself and love yourself unconditionally. You're doing the best with the knowledge you have.

Raising Children

This chapter takes a bit of a different spin. I speak about raising teens and the challenges that may come with this stage of life. I am not yet raising a teen; however, through my observations from my current career along with research, I have formed opinions about how I may choose to raise my teenage girl. There are so many different types of parents in the world. There are the parents who hover, monitor, and protect their child from almost everything; they are also known as helicopter parents. There are authoritarian parents who tend to use the words "because I said so," make rules, enforce consequences, and inflict punishment. There are permissive parents who typically play more of a friend role than that of a parent, and they tend to only step in when serious issues arise with their children. Pay attention to the type of parenting style you possess and ask yourself if it is working for you and your children. If you don't feel that your current style is effective, then it's never too late to pick up a few tricks and make a few change-ups. That's the beautiful thing about parenting: you're never done being a parent. Your style just shifts as the child ages from baby to toddler to teen to adult.

I personally am a believer of natural consequences. For example, if my school-aged child leaves their lunch at home in the fridge after I have reminded them to bring it, I would give them a pass the first time and bring the lunch to the school. However, if the child continues to forget their lunch after being reminded,

I would simply say, "Sorry, kid; I love you, but I know you have the skills to figure it out on your own" as Barbara Coloroso would say. I promise you they won't starve. If anything, they will be resourceful and source out food from the office or from fellow classmates. This might seem harsh to some of you reading, but I believe that this will teach the kid how to become self-reliant and independent. It will also teach them that if they don't want to be hungry, they need to remember to bring their lunch in the morning before leaving for school. This might just mean that they need to write a note for themselves or that they need to buy a brightly coloured lunch bag that catches their eye when they open the fridge. I'm not about punishing my kids. I don't believe that grounding them in their room for a month is effective. I would rather have a conversation, talk it out with the child, and empower the child to come to grips with what has been done and own it, learn from it, and move forward. Also, as the parent, you need to be willing to commit to the punishment you are dishing out. As Barbara Coloroso would say, "If you ground them for a month, you are also grounding yourself for that month as you will be the one stuck at home with them."

I'm just thinking out loud here. This is how I picture myself raising my child. These are all fantasies at the moment as I'm not actually in this phase of life. I might get an eye-opening experience myself when I get there.

I'm thinking about the good old chores that we all love… Well, some people actually love cleaning and that's A-Okay. When it comes to chores, I think I will make a chore list to hang on the wall. I'm thinking that I would like to do some type of reward system that involves a reward for the entire family, not just the child. If chores are all completed by Friday, then we can have a family outing to the movies or to the park. If chores are not completed by Friday, then the whole family suffers and no one gets to enjoy an outing. In my brain, I believe that this will build a sense of teamwork within the child and family. Everyone needs to work together to do their part before going on a fun family outing. I am also the person who says it's not the end of the world if the kid forgets to make their bed one day. See, I'm just venting my ideas here. In my head, in a perfect world, this is how I picture raising a toddler and a teen. But who knows how the fuck I will parent until I actually get to that stage? I might just end up saying, "Fuck the chore list; if it gets done, it gets done." If you'd like some information about parenting, Barbara Coloroso's work is brilliant. She really makes sense of the whole parenting thing from a new perspective. I love her famous saying, "There is no problem so great it can't be solved." I also recommend following Cat and Nat on social media if you are more of a "wing it, I'm doing the best damn job possible" kind of mom. They wrote a book called *Mom Truths* which got me through my pregnancy. They give a reality check to moms and remind us that it's okay to fuck up and that you are doing the best you can. You'll get a good chuckle and they will remind you that you are doing the hardest job on the planet, being a parent.

These are my commitments to my kiddos. I am going to show up for you on a daily basis. Showing up for me means being present and letting my kids know that I am a consistent, safe person in their life who will listen intently. Showing up for my child also means that I will be an ear for them always, they will feel validated, and Mom will only be a phone call away. Showing up means the laundry or dishes can wait if my kiddo needs a good chat with Mom. Kids need consistency. If you say something, then follow through with it; this will teach the kid honesty, and it will let them know that you mean what you say and say what you mean. Now, as mentioned, you all have your own ways of parenting, so don't lose your shit on me for having mine. My kids will know what death is, my kids will know what sex is, my kids will see and help the homeless by prepping a meal before Christmas. I want my kids to appreciate what they have but recognize that not everyone is that fortunate. Gratitude is a beautiful thing. We can word things in kid-friendly ways to teach them about the realities of the world. I believe that sheltering children to try and protect their feelings from getting hurt is only going to leave them feeling confused in the long run. At the end of the day, my goal is to raise respectful, kind-hearted human beings who can make decisions for themselves and who learn the appropriate information for their age about sex, death, etc. from their parent and not from a peer at school. Because let's face it: kids are going to learn things from peers. We can't stop that. Our kids are at school in the presence of teachers and peers for more of their life than they are at home. They are bound to learn some fucked up shit, so if I can help it, I want to make sure my kids are getting the correct information from a reliable source, aka Mom.

This can be a scary-ass world to raise children in. When I was a child, I never heard about murders or kidnappings in my home town. Nowadays, it's rare to go a week without hearing about a shooting in my home town. How are we keeping our kids safe if we are not talking about these realities? I am thankful for my mother for teaching me right from wrong and for recognizing danger in my surroundings. I was not a sheltered child, and I was allowed to travel to foreign countries with friends. I knew about street smarts; I always walked home with my brother from school (the buddy system). Kids need to learn to make decisions for themselves, but they also need the proper information and resources from us, their parents, in order to make those tough decisions. Too often we are waiting for people to make decisions on our behalf; many of us can't think for ourselves. Let's empower our children to make decisions and learn from mistakes instead of telling them what to do and how to think. Let the kids do a load of laundry; let the kids have a sleepover at their friend's house (of course meet the parents first); let the kids go to the party. Let kids be kids. Let mistakes happen, and be there to cheer them on or talk them through their decisions. I want to be the parent that my kid can call at any time of day or night. I want my kid to know that I will not judge them;

I will only hear them out, support, and encourage. It won't always be a bed of roses. I will use tough love when appropriate.

Speaking of the world being a scary place, it's crazy to know that kids can get drugs from a random person on the street. Drugs are so accessible these days, and let's face it: our kids are most likely going to experiment with a few in their lifetime. It's important that we talk to our teens and young adults about substance use, and the effects and consequences that come along with this. Education is everything. I grew up playing competitive sports, and so experimenting with drugs was not appealing to me in the slightest. I focused all of my energy on health and fitness as opposed to snorting something up my nose like most of the people in my high school were doing. Most people say that the teen years are the worst years for parents. I have had the wonderful opportunity to work with high risk youth in my positions and I love teenagers, and the more badass, the better, for me. I'm not at all saying I want my kid to be a bas-ass punk, I'm just saying this is where my expertise lies and I feel confident in my abilities to work with them. A teenager will tell you how it is. They will let you know what's on their mind OR they won't. Just as it is difficult to figure out your baby's cries, it can also be challenging to reach your teen who may be isolating themselves. Personally, I would take a teen who is feeling isolated over the crying baby stage anytime. Babies rely on you for everything, yet they can't tell you anything. I didn't have a lot of experience with babies growing up; therefore, prior to having my own, you could say I was very inexperienced. Luckily, it's different when it's your own child versus someone else's, and to this day, I am absolutely making shit up as I go and pretending like I know what the fuck I am doing as a mother to a young baby.

Our kids need us to be on their team. They need to see us in the stands at their hockey games, and they need us to show up when they are hurt or in trouble. In a world where bullying happens not only in the schools but online, it's important that we support our children and take time to listen to their emotions, thoughts, and feelings. "Kids need to know that they are believed in, they are trusted, they are important, they are listened to and they are cared for" – Barbara Coloroso. Teach your kids to stand up and support one another. Teach your kids to stand up to the bully. Kids should not be fearful of going to school. Let's work together to ensure that our children have a voice at home, at school, in the workplace, and wherever their journey may take them in life. We need to teach our children that their voices are powerful and that they matter.

Children deserve to be loved unconditionally through the good and the bad. They need to feel safe and supported. Their basic needs have to be met in order for them to grasp any other concept in their lives. Children need to develop a sense of self-worth. Children are mirrors of what they witness in the household. A child will likely possess and outwardly express anger if they constantly see their parents arguing and name-calling. Children will learn to be affectionate if they see their parents bonding and connecting through appropriate physical touch (hugs and kisses).

It's important to give your children space. Each and every one of us has a body. That means that each and every one of us has a right to boundaries for our bodies. Children should not be forced to hug extended family members if they don't want to. We need to teach children the importance of privacy and that their bodies are sacred and people don't have permission to touch them, grab them, or look at them inappropriately. We need to teach our children how to budget, save, and do taxes. Enough with the bullshit long division in school; we have calculators for a reason. Let's teach our children real-life skills that they will use and learn throughout their entire lifetime. Let's teach our children how to be respectful, nice people. Let's teach our children that there is no dream too big or too unrealistic that they can't conquer.

Lesson number eight: Your children have a voice, so stop and listen to them. Your kiddos are little sponges and will soak up any and all information heard, seen, and told. Raise respectful, kind-hearted kids and help make the world a better place.

Testing 123

I'm guessing that some of you mushy people want to know how my fiancé and I met, fell in love, yada, yada, yada. I had just broken it off with my ex, and I was on the phone with my psychic (which I will get into later in the book). My psychic mentioned that I now had a free soul. She told me that she saw me finding a man very quickly, settling down, having kids, etc., and that this is what my soul craved/needed. I thought to myself, "There is no way that I am getting into a relationship right away. I don't know any men out here, and the men I do know are happily married." Well, two weeks after my ex and I broke up, I walked past this handsome man in the park while we were walking our dogs. We exchanged smiles and continued walking, but I cannot explain in words the energy that moved through my body while passing him by. I continued to think about him and his smile throughout my walk, and something in me told me that I "needed to know him." I went home and wrote my gratitude list, and on that list, I wrote "guy in park with dog."

After this initial moment, we continued to walk by one another on an almost daily basis for a couple of weeks. We would smile at one another and continue walking. I would talk about this guy in the park with his dog to my friends without even knowing his name. One day, we both thought enough is enough; we're going to introduce ourselves. We walked together in the park that night, getting to know one another. I finally found out what his name was and that his dog's name was Duke. I was excited that I could actually write their names on my gratitude list instead of "guy in park with dog." You'll immediately know if you connect with someone and their values based off of some of the questions that are asked. I remember so vividly him asking me if I was interested in having children. Boom, we found one thing in common. "He's a family man," I thought to myself. Then we spoke about careers, and boom, we found our second thing in common: "He's a hard worker and a manager of a peat moss company," I thought to myself. I also thought, "What the fuck is Peat?" (I definitely had to go home and do some research.) Then he asked how old I was and when I answered, I could instantly see the expression on his face change from happy to worried. He told me that he thought I looked older, and then he explained that he was ten years older than me. In that moment, age didn't faze me one bit because I was so intrigued by this man who had similar values as myself.

He worked up the courage to ask me out on a date, and we continued to get to know one another. Six months later, we were engaged, and I had moved in with him and Duke. Nine months after meeting, we conceived our first child together. I know some of you are thinking, "Holy fuck, girl; that's all too fast." And I'm asking you, "Too fast for who?" You? Social media? The parents? Whose timeline are you on? Who are you trying to impress or please? Haters will hate and people will judge; let them! That's about them and their issues, not yours. Why the fuck does society have expectations? Better yet, why the fuck do people choose to follow those expectations? Marry who you want to marry, when you choose to do so. Have children, don't have children, go to university, drop out. Who gives a shit, as long as you are happy and you are living your life? It's your damn life. Don't let anyone try to control it, alter it, or influence it. The universe has its own timeline and its own journey set out for you.

At this point in my life, I was looking to settle down with my forever person. My whole life, that's all I craved: my forever relationship. So yes, fast for some of you, and just perfect for me at the time. I learned in life that I don't owe explanations to people. This is my life. We get one life that we know of. Do what you want with it. Marry and love who you want to. Life is too short to wake up with regrets. My psychic was right, once again (she's always right). I had found my man, and quickly. And no, our relationship is not perfect, and I am telling you now that a baby will give any relationship a few hiccups to overcome. Only you and that person get to decide whether or not you will make it through life's corkscrews together.

I know that you have heard how important communication is in relationships. I know very well that in my intimate relationships, I am not good at communicating, and I own that. It's almost as if I think my partner should read my mind, like what the fuck, buddy, you don't know what I'm thinking 24/7? I have learned that if you have something on your mind, you shouldn't be fearful to share this with your partner and you shouldn't be fearful of the response from your partner. Yes, your partner might get defensive or upset in the moment, but allowing your emotions to bottle up to a point of explosion is far worse than your partner feeling a little upset in the moment.

I am telling you that a baby will test your communication skills. If you don't express your needs, wants, and desires to your partner, they aren't going to know, because in reality they actually aren't mind readers as much as we would like them to be. Life would be soooooo much easier if men could get inside women's brains. Am I right, ladies? Life would go something like this:

> Husband: Hello, my beautiful wife who I love to pieces, why don't you go upstairs and run a hot bath for yourself while I make dinner, feed the baby, and fold the laundry (because we all know that your laundry sits for two weeks after it's washed, lol)? I booked a vacation just for you

and your best friend to get away for a weekend because I know how much you deserve it.

As much as I joke about this, you also need to know that his needs matter, too. You should take care of and pamper each other. You will be less resentful and more appreciative if you meet the other person where they are at. If you can both get good at recognizing when the other is struggling and then step in to offer your support, you'll be surprised how smooth the relationship will be, even with a crying baby added into the mix. Express your needs. Share your passions and your visions with this person and build an empire together.

I truly believe that there is someone out there for everyone. I also believe that the universe will let you know when the time is right to find your person. Pay attention to the things taking place around you, and don't overthink or question what the universe offers you. And for God's sake, don't settle. Don't live by society's norms in fear of being judged. Shout-out to all of you who have found your match, your ride or die, your soulmate. Go and scream it from a mountain top, elope, have a grand wedding, or don't get married at all. All I ask is that you do what your heart desires, and don't for a second try to please anyone else but yourself. Your relationship is for you and your partner only. People will expect you to involve them in wedding planning, people will expect you to have children after marriage, people will expect you to give yourself a break in between partners. Well, I have an instruction for all of those people judging: Worry about your own goddamn life and your own fucking happiness instead of someone else's.

Allow yourself to love and be loved. Cherish the love between one another. Don't allow jealousy to take over. You chose each other; honour that. Make sure to laugh with your mate, love deeply, and fully accept one another for who they are. You can't change a damn thing about them, and why would you want to? Their quirks and personality traits make them who the universe intended them to be. Say I love you every morning, noon and night. "Keep the expectation of your relationship real. In other words, recognize that one person cannot fulfil everything in you, that's what friendships are for" – Vesna Bailey. Make sure you and your lover book a date night at least once a month; you owe that to yourselves. My relationship with my partner has not been a bed of roses. I'd say our relationship has been more like a daily cliff-jump since having a baby. Regardless of whatever happens between my partner and I, we created a human life together and I will forever love him and cherish him for that.

In the event that a couple does end their relationship for whatever reason, I hope there is no hatred. I hope there is no anger or regret. I hope there are only lessons learned. I hope there is forgiveness and love, even if it's no longer the romantic type of love. I hope you're able to look back on your memories and cherish the good times with one another. Sometimes people grow apart, and that is okay. Maybe they were only meant to be on your journey for so long to teach you something, maybe to tell yourself that you require more self-love. There are reasons why we get into romantic relationships with one another (there is some form of attachment, connection, bond, etc.). Only you have the ability to figure out if a relationship is best for you or not. You need to learn this on your own. I'm not going to sit here and tell you to leave if you're not ready, because you will decide that on your own terms. However, I will not condone or applaud abuse of any sort. I hope you find the strength inside of your being to leave an abusive relationship of any kind. You're a beautiful creation, and you deserve the very best in life. Everyone deserves to be loved.

As mentioned in the first chapter of this book, I dove headfirst into all of my relationships. I went into each of them with the sole purpose for them "to complete me" and keep me secure. I am not afraid to admit to all of you that I have insecurities. I am afraid to be alone. I accept love from pretty much anyone who will provide it, because I crave love. I lost some meaningful relationships in my life at a young age. I'm not using my abandonment as an excuse for my choices, and I don't regret my choices, but I longed so badly for a loving, compassionate partner that I didn't provide myself with enough solitude to love me.

I have only finally realized that I have been a broken record on repeat. I came to this realization when I had a good conversation with a friend after having my daughter. This person told me that the universe would continue to put me in the same scenario over and over until I was ready to learn the lesson I needed to learn. What is the lesson, you ask? After processing, I have come to the conclusion that I continue to fall into the same pattern with each person I enter into a relationship with. Let me explain my pattern. I meet someone and immediately fall in love with the idea of that person. I dive headfirst into the relationship and put all of my eggs into the relationship basket. It's fun and good for a while and then my love fades out. So, did I even love them in the first place, or was I trying too desperately to find an easy replacement for the feeling of abandonment within myself? I get to a place where I get too comfortable, I get bored, and I realize some of the qualities within these people are not even close to what I was searching for. I leave the relationship and jump right back into the next best thing in front of me at the time. In saying this, I truly believe that my partner is my soulmate. We dove headfirst into everything but he balances me, he supports me and he desires me. Now I just need to look my damn self in the mirror every day and say "Alysha, you are deserving of his love and he's not going to hurt you".

I'm going to be extremely honest with you guys right now. Having a baby has put me in a state of unhappiness, confusion and I have felt lost. I completed another reading with my psychic in February in desperation to get some answers and clarity about my life and some decisions that lie in front of me. She reassured me that my man loves me deeply. She told me that the greatest form of intimacy is listening. Listening to what each soul needs and desires and respecting it opposed to trying to change or control it.

She mentioned that our relationship got a bit off track but if we are able to clean up the debris and leave the past in the past that we will have a prosperous life full of love together. She told me that we need to experience solitude together. This brought me to tears because the first four months of my daughter's life, I kept telling myself that I needed to experience solitude alone when really, I need "solitude" time together with my partner to re-connect.

Love can be a complicated thing if you don't fall in love with yourself first. In this moment, I appreciate my life, I am grateful for my partner and my daughter, and I am taking it one day at a time, reminding myself to stay present and not focus so much on the future. I need to allow myself to heal and forgive in order to move forward. This is a reminder to myself that love conquers all.

Lesson number nine: You are all worthy of love. Don't for a second think otherwise!
Quit judging one another and quit comparing your relationships and the unrealistic shit you see on social media, and live for you.

The Universe

Have you ever gone through with something that you knew in your gut wasn't right, wasn't true to your heart? We have this little thing called intuition. If we take it seriously and get to know and respect it, our intuition will do wonders for our life. This chapter might leave some of you feeling skeptical, and that's fine. I'm not here to try and sway your opinions or beliefs. We all have different beliefs, and that's okay. I'm just happy that you believe in something!

I want to talk about believing in yourself; believing in yourself when no one else believes in you; believing in yourself and your visions so profoundly that nothing on this planet can stop you; believing in yourself and your vision so deeply that you wake up feeling inspired. I challenge you to stop for a minute and take a really good look at your life. Do you feel like you are just going through the motions of life? Do you have to snooze the alarm fifty times before you get out of bed? Do you struggle just to get out of bed in general? I want you to find your purpose on this planet. "The two most important days in your life are the day you are born and the day you find out WHY" – Lewis Mocker. What is your WHY in life? What motivates you? What fuels your inner soul? When you can answer these questions honestly, then I ask you, what lengths will you go to fight and protect your mission, your vision, your purpose?

The universe will provide you with opportunity, it will provide you with experiences for growth, it will challenge you, and it will support you. The beautiful thing about the universe is that it is always working for you. Start paying attention to the people you attract into your life, to your self-talk/thoughts, to your conversations with others. Do they tend to be positive or negative? Are they supporting or hindering your growth in life? The human race has a scary amount of potential. I often hear people say that they want to leave their 9-5 job and work from home, be a stay-at-home parent, travel, and have nice things, but they do not actually put forth the time or energy into making it happen, and the belief is not present. They get comfortable with settling. I'm telling you right now that if you have a passion and you know your purpose on this planet, absolutely nothing will stop you from attaining your goals. "The most expensive thing in the world is a missed opportunity" – Rachel Bell. So, when the universe hands you an opportunity, grab it with both hands, secure it, and run with it. Be selfish with your time and energy and put it into your goals, your visions for yourself, and your family.

It's easy to become comfortable in a world that has "societal expectations" of how we should feel and act. Being comfortable and settling when we are unhappy is not what we were put on this planet to do. The amount of wasted talent of those who choose to settle and go through the motions of life is sad. Stepping out of your comfort zone and being told no is extremely hard. The reality is you will be told no by a lot of people, but I can promise you that if you believe in yourself one hundred per cent, those noes turn to yeses and will motivate you that much more. You can let the noes of the world bring you down. You can have a self-pity party, but it won't move you ahead. That's for damn sure. If you have a fucking dream, I dare you to make it become reality.

Stop fucking comparing yourself to others. You are unique and no one on Earth has the same genetic makeup as you do. Isn't that absolutely insanely wonderful! There is only one you, and you have every opportunity in the palm of your hand. Why are you comparing yourself to your friend, to your dad, to your boss, to your favourite hockey player? Shift your self-talk away from comparison and focus it on you, your abilities, and your visions, and then make them fucking happen. If you have to find something to motivate you to put in the work, then you are not being true to yourself and you're trying to live someone else's reality. We all have a set of values that makes us unique. Just be honest with yourself about what yours are and then begin to really live in your values on a daily basis. You are who you are. If you value money, that is not a bad thing; that is your value, and there is nothing wrong with that. If you value family, that is not a bad thing; that is your value, and there is nothing wrong with that. It becomes a problem when you expect someone else to live outside of their true values.

Stop making excuses. Some of my favourites are: "I don't have enough time," (MAKE TIME!); "I don't have enough money," (SAVE MONEY!); "I'm afraid I might fail," (YES, YOU PROBABLY WILL, but get back up and try again!); and "I'm afraid to be told no," (YOU WILL ONE HUNDRED AND TEN PER CENT be told no a million times, but it only takes one yes to make a difference). These excuses are actually your brain's way of getting you to settle and remain stuck inside of your comfort zone. It is natural for our brains to bring us back to certainty. Well, I am telling you right fucking now there is no such thing as certainty. It is not certain that you will have a job tomorrow. It is not certain that you will be able to have children. It is not certain that tomorrow will even come. So, stop wasting time by making excuses and take action. Get in the driver's seat, put on your fucking seat belt, and drive. Don't let anyone or anything stop you and your vision. The universe has endless amounts of opportunity. Your staircase is limitless.

If you believe in yourself and your vision so badly, then there is NO need for a plan B. If you tell yourself that a plan B exists, you are secretly telling yourself that you do not fully believe in yourself or your abilities to make your visions reality. "What you think about, you bring about" – Dr. John Demartini. Allow your thoughts to enter into the universe and be ready for the universe to give you what you want in return. You must have an open mind. You must have a willingness to learn and to bloom. Find mentors, listen to podcasts, read books, surround yourself with like-minded people, and your Plan A (your only plan) will come through for you.

I obtained a bachelor's degree in social work from university. Do I regret attending school? Absolutely not! I know my purpose on this planet is to help people, but I also know that my purpose in life is more than sitting behind a desk, completing paperwork, and working a 9-5 job. This is called settling, in my world, and I am choosing not to settle. Some people love their 9-5 job, and I am not downing these individuals. The point I am trying to get across is this: find something that you absolutely can't wait to wake up in the morning to do and do it. Find happiness in your day by making the effort to create it. Instead of telling yourself "I'm not qualified enough for that position," or "This person is way smarter than me," change your self-talk and take the leap; better yet, believe in yourself while taking the leap. Bottom line: if you're not fucking happy with your life, then change it. You are the driver of your life, so buy the fucking plane ticket, quit the shitty job, or open the hair salon you have talked about your entire life. Just do it.

Our brains try to protect us by keeping us comfortable. Our brains convince us to stay put and settle because it's "safe." If you have a dream, fuck staying safe. You need to go after it like the world is on fire. If someone challenges you or laughs at your dream, allow that to push you even further and motivate you even more to accomplish your dreams. I'm telling you that once you know what your purpose on this planet is, you won't need anyone to validate you; you won't need anyone to cheer you on, because you will possess enough of that within yourself to accomplish your goal. The reality is, whatever goals you set for yourself, whatever visions you chose to make reality, there will always be someone in the crowd criticizing you. The truth is, you will never be criticized by someone focusing on their dreams and doing more than you. A wise mentor of mine always says "someone else's opinion of my is NONE of my business" -Rachel Hollis and her therapist. I live and breath this on a daily basis because so long as I am physically on this earth, I'm going to make a difference and live out my purpose in this world with or without your criticism or opinions of me.

I have had a ton of business opportunities presented to me over the past few years, including Arbonne, Amway, Young Living, and HempWorx to name a few. I kept asking myself and the universe why I was being presented with these networking business opportunities. The answer I came up with was I needed to meet and surround myself with like-minded, dedicated, hardworking individuals who were committed to making their dreams become reality. These individuals showed me what life could be like when you obtain financial freedom. These individuals showed me what staying at home with the children while running a badass business could look like. I knew that I wanted that, so I was open to trying anything that would get me there. However, I realized after about one year of owning my Arbonne business that this was not my passion; it was not my purpose. I loved the product and used the product on a daily basis, but I knew in my heart that this was not my answer to financial freedom. I knew that I was not passionate about this business. I thank the universe for providing me with these opportunities and surrounding me with beautiful souls who, like me, wanted to continue to grow and serve others. I have realized during my mat leave that my purpose on this planet is to write this book and the books that will follow and to become a certified Life Coach. This realization punched me square in the face after the birth of my daughter and it opened my eyes to the opportunities that lay in front of me. Having my baby girl made me realize that I don't want to work for someone the rest of my life. I am building my own empire, one that includes supporting others on their journeys and one that allows me to still be home with my little bean to watch her flourish and grow.

As I sit here and write this book, I am actually freeing myself of anything that my soul has carried and been unable to let go of. As I sit here and write this book, I imagine myself standing on a stage, talking about my book to thousands of people; I imagine myself standing in front of bookstores doing meet-and-greets; I imagine myself travelling to speak in front of audiences all over the world; I imagine a series of books I will write and all of the opportunities that the universe is providing me with. I literally cannot wait to wake up in the morning and get the baby fed and ready for the day and back to sleep so I can sit and write my book. Writing brings me joy. Writing feels freeing. I am leaving all of my current knowledge on these pages for you to use in your own life if you choose to do so. As a little girl, I wrote letters to friends and family members which all came directly from my heart on to the page. Now, I am passionate about spreading my messages on a larger scale, and so I used my mat leave time to write and publish my first book. My purpose in life has always been to serve and support people. This book has allowed me to release some of my own pain, knowledge, and life lessons in order to hopefully help you, the reader, in some shape or form. My work is not done after this book. This book is only the beginning. It is one of my *New Beginnings.*

Whatever your vision is, when you discover your purpose, your why, protect it with everything inside of you and don't let anyone's opinions or thoughts stop you. You are responsible for your own happiness. You create it, attract it, manifest it. You are the architect of your reality. You choose the thoughts, the perceptions, and your reactions to external forces. You possess all of the tools needed to expand your awareness, to choose happiness, to choose love. You are that powerful. Create the life you deserve. Stop waiting for the time to be right, stop waiting for the promotion, stop waiting for tomorrow. START today, right now. Just do something today that your future self will thank you for. If you were on your deathbed, would you honestly be happy with the life you have lived? Would you have regrets? Would you wish for time travel to go back and re-do something? If the answer is yes, then I encourage you to start looking deep within your soul to figure out your purpose on this planet. Be brutally honest with yourself and your answers. I got serious with myself on mat leave and asked, "Alysha, if you died tomorrow would you be content with your accomplishments and failures?" My answer was "Heck no." So, I wrote my visions on a piece of scrap paper and then… I simply ACTED on my visions. I took the fucking leap. I began to write. As I continued to write, I experienced tears of gratitude and said, "I'm going to make a difference to someone in this world." It doesn't matter to me if it is one person or fifty. By writing, I just knew that I would make some sort of impact upon someone in this world. And that alone lit my soul on fire.

Lesson number ten: Trust the timing of your life.

> *Your work is going to fill a large part of your life and the only way to be truly satisfied is to do what you believe is great work. And the only way to do great work is to love what you do. If you haven't found it yet, keep looking. Don't settle. As with all matters of the heart, you'll know when you find it. – Steve Jobs*

Becoming Grounded

Gratitude is very powerful, and if you implement it into your daily life, I can guarantee that your life will look a little different. Writing a gratitude list is one of many ways that you can practice incorporating gratitude and appreciation into your life. It's a rather simple process: grab a piece of paper and a pen and just starting writing everything and anything that comes to mind that you are thankful for in your life. You'd be surprised how fast the page fills once you start writing.

Go out, buy a journal for yourself, and take a few minutes every day to write your gratitude list. Do this for one year and see how it impacts your life and perspective. I tell myself every day that I get to wake up how lucky I am to be alive. It is difficult in a busy world to be present and live from moment to moment. A lot of the time we are so focused on the past or future that we forget to enjoy moments on a daily basis. Make the time to call your grandparents, make the time to meditate, make the time to reflect, make the time to read or do something to support your growth. I understand you might work 9-5 and then run home with McDonald's for dinner to get the kids out the door for hockey practice. I understand that your boss might have asked you to work overtime and you're dead tired at the end of the day. But make a conscious effort to take a few minutes out of each day to develop yourself, to heal yourself, and to love yourself; I promise you won't regret this.

There are apps for everything nowadays. Pull out your phone and download a meditation app, or download a gratitude journal or an exercise app. If you're type A personality and need to write out what your day looks like in the calendar, pencil in time for you, pencil in time for gratitude. There are so many unfortunate things in this world that occur on a daily basis and are out of our control. My Nan always looks at the positive in everything. She always tells me, "There are people much worse off. When something goes wrong in my life, I feel guilty to complain because I look at people who have it much worse than I do and it changes my perspective." Focus on you and the things you can control, and make sure to be thankful for these things on a daily basis. Don't allow yourself to become too busy or so caught up with pointless, mundane daily tasks that you forget to give your children a hug before bed or you forget to tell your partner that you love them or you forget to feed the dog. The hard reality is we don't know when our last physical day on Earth will be, but if we can live for moments, and become present, then we won't regret not slowing down to make the phone call. We won't regret not slowing down to practice self-care.

Gratitude can look different for everyone. It can look like prayer, it can look like a list, or you can speak out loud to loved ones who have passed. There is no correct way to display gratitude. All I know is by incorporating gratitude into my life, my perspective has shifted from "Poor me" and complaints to "It's a great day to be alive; I get another day to live my purpose." I choose to meditate and express my gratitude to my loved ones who have passed over, get psychic readings every six months, and go to reiki for self-care. I meditate in my daughter's nursery as I find it very peaceful. I lay on the floor, surround myself with my crystals, play soft piano music, close my eyes, and talk with Peter and Bob. I focus on my breathing; I focus on quieting my mind and listening to any messages that my loved ones provide me with.

It is comforting to know that Bob and Peter are always by my side. They are constantly making my baby girl laugh, which makes sense because they were jokesters in the physical world. I'll catch her looking up into the corner and smiling while cooing, and I'll always say, "Are Peter and Grandpa making you laugh?" Some of you reading might be skeptical, might not believe in psychics, and might not believe in life after death, and that's fine. You're entitled to your own beliefs.

On October 18th, 2019 I completed a reading via telephone with my psychic. She explained that Peter and Bob had both stepped forward to pass along information to me. This particular reading was very interesting because she asked me if I was in the process of writing something (I had only begun the first chapter and the titles of my book prior to speaking with her). She proceeded to ask if what I was writing would be a series. My psychic talked about my book and my success for an entire hour over the phone. Peter and Bob believe in me so profoundly from the other side that they wouldn't allow my psychic to move on to other topics. She expressed that I needed to write this book right now and that the universe needed this book published to support people through their own journeys of healing. This moment confirmed for me that this was my purpose; this was my calling in life. I have always loved to write and I just instantly knew that I wanted to write a book that people could relate too. Thank you for taking time out of your busy day to read my book. You are such an important part of my journey.

If today was your last day on this planet, would you be satisfied? If the answer is no, then you have some re-evaluating to do. Life is too damn short and we are not promised a tomorrow, so what are you waiting for? It does not matter what age you are; if you are reading this and you are not pleased with the life you're living, if you don't wake up every morning and say "Fuck, it's a great day to be alive and I love what I do," then please look within and ask yourself why you are settling for the life you're currently living. You have potential within; you just need to believe it with all your soul.

To all of you who are taking the time to read my book, I hope you are getting something out of it, whether it be a laugh, a life lesson, or motivation. I can't thank you enough for supporting me. I think the underlying message throughout my book is "DON'T SETTLE." Life is what you make of it. Whatever has happened to you has helped shape the person you are today. You get to decide how to live your life each day. You get to decide your mood. You get to decide how to react to the nonsense of the world. You are important, you matter, and I love each and every one of you.

To close out this chapter, I want to speak about where the inspiration of my cover for this book came from. The mountains are my favourite place in the entire world, and they help keep me grounded. Mountains are so pure. They change gradually over time, but with these changes they are able to remain true to what they are even while enduring massive amounts of bullshit (weather, snow, wind). They always manage to stand tall and strong. The mountains are my safe place. They help keep me inspired and remind me to live in moments. No mountain is identical to another, and this makes me appreciate the beauty and uniqueness of each. They remind me that sometimes life will throw you lemons and require you to climb that mountain, but maintain hope in knowing that the other side of the mountain will be bright and will bring you closer to the sun (your happiness). For when I look up at the snow-topped peaks, I think, "How brave I am to have come this far. To keep going, push past my peak. I will never know what's waiting for me on the other side if I don't proceed." Choose to view that mountain as an opportunity awaiting rather than a challenge too grand to conquer.

Lesson number eleven:

> *Anything that annoys you is teaching you patience.*
> *Anyone who abandons you is teaching you how to*
> *stand on your own two feet. Anything that angers you*

is teaching you forgiveness and compassion. Anything that has power over you is teaching you how to take the power back. Anything that you hate is teaching you unconditional love, anything that you fear is teaching you courage to overcome it, anything you can't control is teaching you how to let go and trust the universe. – Amy Sangster

You Got This

I feel like you are going through some hard times right now. Maybe that's why you bought this book? Anyways, this chapter is dedicated to you. I need you to know you're not alone. I care about you and I am sending love and positivity your way. When you feel like the world is crumbling beneath you, I need you to remind yourself that you matter. You are a beautiful human being with a beating heart, a voice, and crazy amounts of potential. Your life matters and today is a new day. Your life is beautiful through my eyes. Your suffering has helped shape who you are and strengthened you to take on the world day by day. I want to help bring you back to this very moment. What is around you? What do you see, smell, and hear? What is this present moment doing for you? What thoughts are running through your mind? I'm reminding you that this very moment is all that exists. The past and the future do not exist in this very moment for you.

I want to help you release some of your pent-up, deep emotions if you'll allow me. I want to try and soothe your soul and give you peace to have a good night's sleep. What you are currently going through doesn't define you; it's actually working in your favour to make you the strongest version of yourself. You are hurting right now, and that is okay, because I believe you will get through this. I'm not exactly sure why this is happening to you, but I have to believe it's to make you, YOU. It's going to hurt for a little while longer, but you are getting there day by day, minute by minute.

Allow me to take on some of your pain right now. I am willing to take some on so that you don't feel you're alone in the process. Vent to me. Right now, stop reading and just vent. Say whatever comes to mind and know that I'm listening. You need to get this off your chest. If you're feeling angry, say "Alysha, I'm fucking angry," and know that it is okay to feel this way for a brief moment. But don't allow the anger to fester. Go for a walk or punch a pillow and then tell yourself you are releasing your pain and moving forward for the remainder of your day. Give yourself ten minutes right now to vent out loud. Say whatever you need to; I'm not judging you.

Do you feel any relief? If yes, then proceed to write a gratitude list right now. Write down everything and anything that comes to mind that you are thankful for. If you are not feeling any relief, then I challenge you to continue venting until you feel even the slightest bit lighter, like you have shed a layer of the onion. What does your self-talk consist of? The things you are saying to yourself will continue to be your truths. I want you to say aloud right now, "I love who I am." I want you to say it again, and again, and again until you fucking believe it!

Stop what you are doing and take a deep breath in, and out. Do this five times. Each time feel your body lighten. Imagine your baggage all packed in your suitcase. Place your suitcase on the conveyor belt and leave it there. Make sure it doesn't have any tags attached to it. Just let it go and let it be. Trust that the universe will dispose of it in the way it needs to. Now, I am asking you to do something extremely hard. Forgive the people who have caused you hurt. You don't have to agree with their actions, but forgiveness is the key to unlocking your own happiness and setting your soul free. Don't allow your attacker or the person who caused you harm to win. If you fall into a victim mentality and stay there, then they are winning. You have your whole life ahead of you. You get to decide right now if you will trust in the process of forgiveness.

The universe is going to continue to show up and challenge you if you don't learn the lesson that it needs you to learn. You will repeat cycles until you learn the lesson. You might get frustrated with yourself and ask, "Why does this keep happening to me?" Well, it's because you haven't yet learned what the universe needs you to learn. That's okay! You'll get there. It might take something drastic and life-changing like bringing a child into the world to learn it, as this is what happened for me. Life is going to be unfair sometimes, period. It's simply what you choose to do with your perceptions that will propel you forward or hold you back. Your soul knows its purpose from the day you are born. It knows exactly what this lifetime is going to bring you, including what you will learn and accomplish. Life has to give each and every one of us challenge in order to test us to see whether we get back on our journey in life or allow this challenge to take us off of the path completely. It's also possible to fall off the path (hit rock bottom) and still climb the rope back to the top, coming out stronger and clearer than ever. Ultimately, perception is key. Instead of viewing things as good or bad, why don't we just view them as they are? They only become positive or negative when we create this perception. For example, your lover cheats on you. You can view this as negative because it hurt you and left you feeling angry, you can view this as positive if you were already looking for an out from the relationship, or you can view this as "It's unfair and shitty that this happened, but it happened and I need to continue living life." You get to decide how to respond to situations.

Please don't stick with something that you are unhappy with, whether that be a job, a relationship, or a type of toothpaste. If your soul isn't meant to be a teacher, for example, the universe will do everything possible to ensure you realize this before your time is up on this physical Earth. You always have a choice, but how do you know if you're making the right one? The universe will always direct you back on to your right path. Your soul purpose is going to be filled with a mixture of trial and errors. Have you ever gotten lost? Ended up in another fucking country, let alone town? How did you get out of this mess? Did you use beautiful technology and Google Maps to get you back on track? You problem-solved, didn't you? Why should it be any different for your life's purpose? You're going to have to come across roadblocks and detours along the way. There is no smooth road, and if there is, it took an extraordinary amount of effort from someone or something to make sure all of the cracks were filled and all of the bumps were paved. Do you ever wonder why your journey keeps bringing you back to the same person, maybe even ten years later? Or back to the same job after you have attempted to leave it multiple times? Maybe we need to stop fighting what is meant to be for us in this lifetime. Of course, if you are unhappy and need a change, I'm not telling you to stay put. You'll actually need to leave in order to recognize where you're meant to be or who you're meant to be with. I know we are always looking for answers as humans. Sometimes, instead of analyzing everything, some things just need to be. You hold all of the answers within your being; you just have to believe it.

Do you sometimes find your energy is being stripped from you? Maybe this is an indicator that your circle needs some adjustments or your career needs a revamp. I have learned to protect my energy. Unpleasant situations and unfulfilling jobs and relationships throughout my life have taught me to cherish my time each and every day. We are all allocated twenty-four hours in a day. Let me make this very clear. Twenty-four hours will pass whether we like it or not. What are you doing in this time frame? We can't control when we die, but we can control how we live when we have the privilege of waking up. Protect your energy and use your time effectively. People will attempt to steal your energy but you have the power to control who your energy is given too. I have arrived at a place in my life where I decide who enters into my life, who stays, and who goes. I create boundaries to protect my energy. My energy is stored for my baby, myself, my family, and my vision. Anything that tries to claim my energy gets a big boot from me. I didn't just wake up one day and say, "Alysha, you deserve to be treated better." This was a gradual process, and it took a lot of hurt and eye-opening experiences to come to this realization. To some, this might be considered selfish. To me, this is considered living my purpose on this planet and fulfilling my destiny.

In life, if there is a problem, address it. "It's usually not the experience itself that is the lesson, it's what you do with the experience" – Ainslie MacLeod. There is always something that you can do to change your situation. If you don't like something, change it. You may ask, "Well, how do I do this?" It's fairly simple. We like to complicate things as humans. Keep it simple, my friend. What are you struggling with? Write it down. Once you have written this, write the steps you need to complete in order to make the change. Once you know your steps, take action on these steps. If you have a goal, write it down in full detail. Write down the action steps. Find mentors with the results you want and then take action. Stop talking about what you want to do and actually do it. "If you have a big enough WHY the HOW'S will take care of themselves" – Dr. John Demartini. Are you limiting yourself? What are your self-limiting beliefs? Write them down and figure out their solutions. I can't say this any louder or any clearer: just act and your visions will begin to manifest around you.

If you're feeling like life is shitty and doing you wrong, I'm asking you to adjust your attitude. Trust me, I have been there feeling sorry for myself and asking, "What have I done to deserve this?" Then my unconscious kicks into gear and says, "Alysha, wake the fuck up." Life isn't going to be a bed of roses, but you get to decide how to react. So, I know you're struggling right now, and that's okay. All I ask is that you don't allow it to fester and follow you day in and day out. Your life is so meaningful. Your life is actually filled with so many beautiful things. You just might not be able to see that right now. Again, that is okay. We will all hit lows in life, but you can choose what to do to get yourself out of it. I believe in you. I love you. You will get through this, even though all you can see is darkness at the moment.

Lesson number twelve: You're going to get stuck; it's inevitable. You will also get through the shitty times because you're an extraordinary person who has the beauty of waking up every day. Be grateful for all that you do have, even in tough times.

Life

The day you come into this world is a gift; it is a miracle; it is pure bliss. To think that you started out as an egg and a sperm and then turned into this beautiful human is remarkable. On the day each of us are born, we are handed unlimited amounts of opportunity and potential. The world is literally at our little fingertips. Can we just take a second to appreciate how fast babies learn? My little bubs was basically holding her own head up at seven weeks old. She had learned that Mom and Dad would come soothe her when she was hangry and that a diaper was always waiting for her when she pooped. Now take everything that babies learn in the first year of their lives (a fucking lot): walking, talking, eating solids. Then imagine the next ninety-nine years of their lives that they can dedicate to learning and growing to become the best version of themselves. Dedicate your New Year's resolution every year to developing and growing a new part of yourself instead of wasting money on a gym membership that you'll never use (unless you already use gym facilities). Learn, grow, take risks, and unite your mind, body, and soul as one. "The mind and body are not separate. What affects one affects the other so take care of yourself." – Shasily

Goddamnit, I can't stress to you enough how beautiful life truly is. We need to take the time to appreciate the little things, celebrate, spread love, and be grateful for every single little thing in our lives. Be grateful for every single soul that enters into your world. Stop fucking complaining!!! There is so much beauty surrounding us. Take a minute right now, wherever you are, to look up at the stars. Look up at the sun or moon and just appreciate your life. Stop being jealous of one another. Stop judging one another. Just love one another. Love doesn't just need to be romantic; spread love and sunshine everywhere you go. A wise soul once told me,

> Be love. Love conquers all and love will free us. The world needs more love. Not lustful, emotional, chemical love, but true love where we as individuals become love and allow it to be a constant thing. – Kyle Americano

Take more pictures; make more memories. Stop buying unnecessary stuff. Your kids don't need every present under the Christmas tree to feel happy. They need constant, unconditional love. Stuff is stuff, but memories and love last a lifetime. One piece of advice that I have learned over time is to pay attention to the things that are said to you that you take offence to. If you become offended about something, it's usually because you know this to be true about yourself. We all have weaknesses and strengths. We are not fucking robots, so just learn to own the things you're good at and the things you're not. These things make you, you. Accepting is the hardest piece. Once you fully accept yourself, you can embrace all that life provides you.

Have gratitude and be thankful for all that you do have. Be thankful for the material items that make life convenient such as an oven, a microwave, a computer, a cell phone. We need to also be thankful for air; for nature; for yesterday and today; for health; for sight, smell, touch, sound, taste; for our vehicles that get us from point A to point B; for clean water; for food; for each other. Let's start to look out for one another and cheer each other on. Let's thank the mailman; let's thank our parents; let's thank our teachers, our doctors, our janitors. We are all one race, and that's HUMAN. Let's treat each other like humans. We all have a pulse, we all have a brain, we have all have a heart. Let's become more aware by using our hearts. Let's stop putting labels on people. Let's start treating people like people. It shouldn't matter where you come from in the world. Slow down, breathe, take a look around you. Have thanks and love deeply.

Allow yourself to be open and honest. Feel every emotion and own it. You will gain more clarity if you quiet your mind and listen. The universe continues to support and challenge us in order to grow. The universe will continue to throw you curveballs until you recognize that there is something you need to learn. Don't dodge or avoid answers because you're scared of the outcome. "Fear arises when we are not living in the current moment but rather in the past or future and neither of these exist" – Kyle Americano. If you catch yourself asking, "Goddamnit, how many times am I going to repeat this? Why don't I learn?", your subconscious self will answer, "As many times as it takes for you to learn."

Don't wake up on your seventy-fifth birthday and regret not taking the chance to write the book. Don't regret not wearing the bikini on the beach because you were scared of people judging your stretch marks. I hope you don't wake up and regret living in silence or not using your imagination to inspire others. "Just in case you haven't heard this for a while: thank you for existing. Thank you for trying every day to feel okay. Thank you for pushing through on your hard days. Thank you for never giving up on yourself." – Anniepositivity

And so, my friends, I will leave you with this: you are all amazing human beings. You all have the potential within to make an impact on this world. Do not let fear stop you from accomplishing your wildest dreams. "Everything in your life happens for a reason. Those reasons support our overall growth and evolution of our souls and spirits" – Kyle Americano. I'm sending positive vibes and love to all. Thanks for taking time out of your precious day to join me on my journey. You have 86,400 seconds each and every day, and so I challenge you to make those seconds count. Don't let life pass you by without giving it your best damn shot.

Guidance from my soul to yours: Make your favourite chapter be the one you are living right now and live for moments! There are so many miracles that surround us on a daily basis, so pay attention. A smile goes a long way, so be the reason for someone's smile. Every damn thing in your life, positive or negative, happens for a reason! Love deeply. Love yourself. Tell your family, your friends, and your co-workers that they are appreciated and that you'll always be an ear for them. Live and breathe your purpose on this planet. BE YOU. If you believe and act, it will be impossible to fail. If you knew success was a certainty, what would you do? "When one door closes another will open in time. This is only preparing you for your grand entrance." – Vesna Bailey

One day you will
tell your story,
of how you've
overcome what
you're going
through now,
and it will become
part of someone
else's survival
guide.

Acknowledgements

I want to take this time to thank each and every individual who has entered into my life. You have supported me through my journey and helped shape the person I am today. I want to particularly thank my brother for being my best friend. I am so proud of you and the man you have become. I'm so excited for you to leave your mark on the world.

I also want to thank my Nanny. I cannot even put into words how much gratitude I have toward you, Nanny. I love you from the bottom of my heart. Our souls are and will always be connected, no matter where we end up. Thank you for spreading love. Thank you for being yourself. Thank you for being a great listener and staying positive during tough times. You are my inspiration and I love you more than words can describe.

A huge thank you to my partner for believing in me and my abilities. Thank you for giving me our beautiful daughter and loving her so deeply.

www.ingramcontent.com/pod-product-compliance
Lightning Source LLC
Chambersburg PA
CBHW031358060726
47590CB00007B/2835